What Readers Are Saying About
The Agile Samurai

Jonathan Rasmusson has written a book for today that captures the excitement and value of what agile software development meant to us at the time of the Agile Manifesto. Look to the master, follow the master, walk with the master, see through the master, become the master.

➤ **Ron Jeffries**
    Coauthor, the Agile Manifesto, www.XProgramming.com

I love books by practitioners who have their hands thoroughly dirty. Jonathan has years of real-world experience with agile, and his book is filled with valuable knowledge. If you're new to agile or want to improve your practice of it, you'd do well to learn from this book.

➤ **Joshua Kerievsky**
    Founder and CEO, Industrial Logic, Inc.

The Agile Samurai is the book I wish I'd read *before* I started my last agile project. The chapters on agile project inception alone are worth the price of admission.

➤ **Michael J. Sikorsky**
    CEO, Robots & Pencils, Inc.

Maybe a few stodgy, grumpy types will turn their noses up at the fun tone. The truth is they don't deserve a book this good.

➤ **Ian Dees**
    Software Engineer

The Agile Samurai helps you steer an agile project from start to finish. No agile toolkit would be complete without this book.

➤ **Wendy Lindemann**
    Agile Program Manager

The Agile Samurai is *exactly* the book you and your team need to understand and deliver using the agile method. It makes the concepts tactile for everyone from the highest level of leadership to the people pushing forward on the front lines.

➤ **Jessica Watson**
   Business Analyst, Shaw Communications

In this book, JR distills his many years of experience in delivering agile projects, with his characteristic warmth, wisdom, and humor. It should be on the reading list for any team looking to adopt agile software delivery. The section on project inceptions alone is required reading for anyone about to undertake a new project (or rescue one that's already in trouble!).

➤ **Dan North**
   Senior Developer, DRW

This book was written with the insight and clarity that can only come from a person who has proved these techniques in the trenches. I have read many books on agile software development; this is by far the most engaging, easy to read, and just plain fun of them all. Get ready to sharpen that sword!

➤ **JP Boodhoo**
   Founder, Develop with Passion

If you want a guide to agile projects backed by real-world success stories and battle scars, read this book. JR brings us an easy and humorous read that covers almost any question you may have on agile and how to make it work. His content is sincere, simple yet comprehensive, realistic, and honest about common pitfalls teams will likely encounter. A great read!

➤ **Eric Liu**
   Lead Consultant, ThoughtWorks

The Agile Samurai

How Agile Masters Deliver Great Software

Jonathan Rasmusson

The Pragmatic Bookshelf

Dallas, Texas • Raleigh, North Carolina

Many of the designations used by manufacturers and sellers to distinguish their products are claimed as trademarks. Where those designations appear in this book, and The Pragmatic Programmers, LLC was aware of a trademark claim, the designations have been printed in initial capital letters or in all capitals. The Pragmatic Starter Kit, The Pragmatic Programmer, Pragmatic Programming, Pragmatic Bookshelf, PragProg and the linking *g* device are trademarks of The Pragmatic Programmers, LLC.

Every precaution was taken in the preparation of this book. However, the publisher assumes no responsibility for errors or omissions, or for damages that may result from the use of information (including program listings) contained herein.

Our Pragmatic courses, workshops, and other products can help you and your team create better software and have more fun. For more information, as well as the latest Pragmatic titles, please visit us at *http://pragprog.com*.

The team that produced this book includes:

Susannah Davidson Pfalzer (editor)
Sara Lynn Eastler (indexer)
Kim Wimpsett (copyeditor)
David J Kelly (typesetter)
Janet Furlow (producer)
Juliet Benda (rights)
Ellie Callahan (support)

Printed in the United States of America.
ISBN-13: 978-1-934356-58-6
Printed on acid-free paper.
Book version: P5.0—April 2014

Contents

Part III — Agile Project Planning

Part IV — Agile Project Execution

Part V — Creating Agile Software

Part VI — Appendixes

Acknowledgments

This book would not have been possible were it not for the love of my life, Tannis, and our wonderful three children, Lucas, Rowan, and Brynn, who supported and loved me every step of the way.

A book like this doesn't happen without a wonderful editor and publisher. Everything quality can be attributed to Susannah Pfalzer. Everything else is mine.

Then there are the pioneering people whose shoulders I merely stand on: Kent Beck, Martin Fowler, Ron Jeffries, Bob Martin, Joshua Kerievsky, Tom and Mary Poppendieck, Kathy Sierra, and the wonderful people at ThoughtWorks.

And of course this book wouldn't be what it is without the incredible feedback and insight generously given from its reviewers and commenters: Noel Rappin, Alan Francis, Kevin Gisi, Jessica Watson, Tomas Gendron, Dave Klein, Michael Sikorsky, Dan North, Janet Gregory, Sanjay Manchiganti, Wendy Lindemann, James Avery, Robin Dymond, Tom Poppendieck, Alice Toth, Ian Dees, Meghan Armstrong, Ram Swaminathan, Heather Karp, Chad Fournier, Matt Hughes, Michael Menard, Tony Semana, Kim Shrier, and Ryheul Kristof. Special thanks also to Kim Wimpsett and Steve Peter for the world-class copy editing and typesetting.

Thank you, Mom and Dad, for your love and encouragement.

And thanks to Dave and Andy for creating a company that lets aspiring young authors create and share their work with the world.

The Agile Samurai—a fierce software-delivery professional capable of dispatching the most dire of software projects, and the toughest delivery schedules, with ease and grace

➤ *Master Sensei*

It's Good to See You

Agile is a way of developing software that reminds us that although computers run the code, it's people who create and maintain it.

It's a framework, attitude, and approach to software delivery that is lean, fast, and pragmatic. It's no silver bullet, but it dramatically increases your chances of success while bringing out the best your team has to offer.

In this book I am going to show you how to crush your agile project. I mean really knock it out of the park. Not only are your projects going to come in on time and on budget, but your customers are actually going to enjoy using the software you create for them, and they are going to love working with you and being part of the process.

Inside, you are going to learn the following:

- How to successfully set up and kick-start your own agile project so clearly that there won't be any confusion as to what your project is about and what it stands for.

- How to gather requirements, estimate, and plan in a clear, open, and honest way.

- How to execute fiercely. You'll learn how to turn your agile project into a well-oiled machine that continuously produces high-quality, production-ready code.

If you're a project lead, this book gives you the tools to set up and lead your agile project from start to finish. If you are an analyst, programmer, tester, UX designer, or project manager, this book gives you the insight and foundation necessary for becoming a valuable agile team member.

How to Read This Book

Feel free to jump to any chapter in the book you want. But if you're looking for how to set things up right from the start, I suggest going through the book from beginning to end.

Part I gives you a brief overview of agile and explains how agile teams work.

Part II introduces one of the most powerful expectation-setting devices your team will have in its arsenal—the inception deck.

Part III is where we get into agile user stories, estimation, and how to build your first agile project plan.

Part IV is all about execution. This is where you learn how to take your plan and turn it into something real—working software your customer can use.

And Part V wraps up by giving you a high-level look at the core agile software engineering practices you're going to need to keep quality up and long-term maintenance costs of your software down.

Fun Bits with Purpose

You can't take this stuff too seriously, and it helps if you can approach the material with a bit of a sense of humor.

To that end, I've lightened things up with pictures, stories, and anecdotes to show you what working on an agile project is like.

War stories take you to the front line of real life agile projects and share some of the successes (and failures) I and others have had while practicing the agile arts.

The *Now you try* exercises are there to snap you out of reading and get you into thinking and doing.

Now you try

Then there is Master Sensei—the legendary agile master experienced and wise in all forms of agile software delivery.

Master Sensei and the aspiring warrior

He will be your guide and spiritual mentor on your agile journey and periodically draw your attention to important agile principles, like this:

Agile principle

Deliver working software frequently, from a couple of weeks to a couple of months, with a preference to the shorter timescale.

He will share with you deeper insight and guidance in how to apply the agile practices.

Online Resources

This book has its own web page, http://pragprog.com/titles/jtrap, where you can find more information about the book and interact in the following ways:

- Participate in a discussion forum with other readers, agile enthusiasts, and me

- Help improve the book by reporting errata, including content suggestions and typos

Let's begin.

Part I

Introducing Agile

CHAPTER 1

Agile in a Nutshell

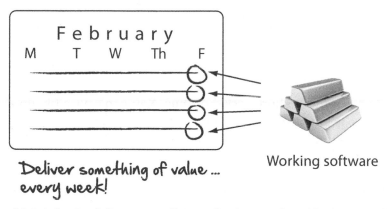

*Deliver something of value ...
every week!*

Working software

What would it take to deliver something of value each and every week?

That's the question we are going to answer in this chapter. By finding out what software delivery looks like through the eyes of our customer, we are going to see how much of what we've traditionally served our customers is waste and how often we've missed what really counts—the regular delivery of working software.

By the end of this chapter, you will have a high-level understanding of agile planning, how we measure success on an agile project, and how the acceptance of three simple truths will enable you to face the tightest of deadlines with courage and the most dire of projects with ease and grace.

1.1   Deliver Something of Value Every Week

Forget about agile for a second, and pretend you are the customer. It's your money and your project, and you've hired a top-notch team to deliver.

What would give you confidence the team you hired was actually delivering? A pile of documentation, plans, and reports? Or the regular delivery of working, tested software made up of your most important features each and every week?

When you start looking at software delivery from your customer's point of view, good things start to happen.

1. You break big problems down into smaller ones.

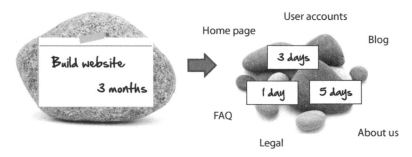

A week is a relatively short period of time. You can't possibly do everything in a week! To get anything done, you have to break big, scary problems down into smaller, simpler, more manageable ones.

2. You focus on the really important stuff and forget everything else.

Most of what we traditionally deliver on software projects is of little or no value to our customer.

Sure, you need documentation. Sure, you need plans. But they are in support of only one thing—working software.

By delivering something of value every week, you are forced to get lean and drop anything that doesn't add value. As a result, you travel lighter and take only what you need.

3. You make sure that what you are delivering works.

Delivering something of value every week implies that what you deliver had better work. That means testing—lots of it, early and often.

No longer something to be sloughed off until the end of the project, daily testing becomes a way of life. The buck stops with you.

4. You go looking for feedback.

How do you know whether you're hitting the bulls-eye if you don't regularly stop and ask your customer if you're aiming at the right target?

Feedback is the headlight that cuts through the fog and keeps you on the road as you're barreling down the highway at 100 miles per hour. Without it, your customer loses the ability to steer—and you end up in the ditch.

5. You change course when necessary.

Original plan

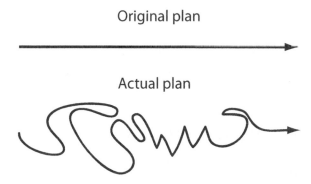

Actual plan

Stuff happens on projects. Things change. What was really important one week can be descoped the next. If you create a plan and follow it blindly, you won't be able to roll with the punches when they come. That's why when reality messes with your plan, you change your plan—not reality.

6. You become accountable.

When you commit to delivering something of value every week and showing your customer how you've spent their money, you become accountable.

- That means owning quality.
- That means owning the schedule.
- That means setting expectations.
- That means spending the money as if it were your own.

- Warning -

Not everyone likes
working this way

Do I think one day everyone is going to be working this way? No way—for the same reason most people don't eat right and exercise.

Delivering something of value every week is not for the faint of heart. It puts the spotlight on you like never before. There is no place to hide. Either you produce something of value or you don't.

But if you like the visibility, have a passion for quality, and have a fierce desire to execute, working on an agile team can be personally very rewarding and a heck of a lot of fun.

And in case the one-week thing is stressing you out, don't worry about it—it's irrelevant. Most agile teams start by delivering something of value every two weeks (really big teams every three).

It's just a metaphor to get you thinking about regularly putting working software in front of your customer, getting some feedback, and changing course when necessary. That's it.

Agile principle

Our highest priority is to satisfy the customer through early and continuous delivery of valuable software.

Let's now take a look at agile planning.

1.2 How Does Agile Planning Work?

Planning an agile project isn't all that much different from preparing for a busy long weekend. Instead of to-do lists and tasks, we use fancy names like *master story lists* and *user stories*.

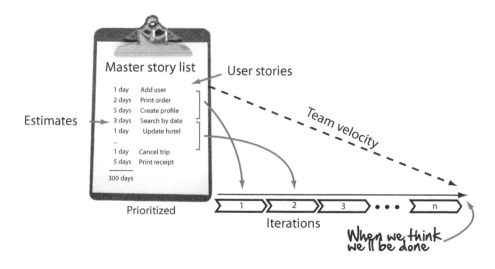

In agile, the *master story list* is your project to-do list. It contains all the high-level features (*user stories*) your customer will want to see in their software. It's prioritized by your customer, it's estimated by your development team, and it forms the basis of your project plan.

The engine for getting stuff done on an agile project is the *iteration*—a one- to two-week period where you take your customers' most important stories and transform them into running, tested software.

Your team members will know how much they can take on by measuring the *team velocity* (how much you can get done per iteration). By tracking your velocity and using it as a predictor of how much you'll get done in the future, you will keep your plans honest and your team from over-committing.

When you and your customer are faced with too much to do, you do the only thing you can—you do less. Being *flexible on scope* is how you'll keep your plan balanced and your commitments real.

And when reality disagrees with your plan, you'll change your plan. *Adaptive planning* is a cornerstone of agile delivery.

That's all there is to agile planning, which we'll cover in much greater depth in Chapter 8, *Agile Planning: Dealing with Reality*, on page 113.

If death is on the line, then you'd better get it done. Just make sure you are sacrificing yourself for a worthy cause and not some unrealistic commitment made more than a year ago at a performance review.

It's true that unrealistic promises do get made and teams are all too often asked to do the impossible. But that doesn't make it right. And continuing the facade of "management by miracle" is a lousy way to run your project and an even worse way to set expectations with your customers.

Working software

With agile, you won't need these kinds of miracles, because you are going to work openly and honestly with your customers from the start—telling it like it is and letting them make the informed decisions about scope, money, and dates.

It's all about choice. You can perpetuate the myth that things will magically turn around. Or you can work with your customer to create plans you can both believe in.

Something else you'll need to know is how agile defines something being done.

1.3 Done Means Done

Say your grandparents hired the neighbor's teenage son to rake and bag the leaves for their front lawn. Would Grandma and Grandpa consider the job done when the teenager did which of the following:

- Produced a report of how he planned to rake the yard?
- Came up with an elegant design?
- Created an elaborate comprehensive test plan?

No way! That kid wouldn't get a dime until the leaves were raked, bagged, and sitting at the side of the house.

In agile, we use the same definition. Delivering a feature in agile means doing everything necessary to produce shippable code.

The analysis, design, coding, testing, and usability experience and design (UX)—it's all there. That doesn't mean we necessarily get every bell and whistle on the first version of a feature or that we push our latest work live at the end of every iteration. But our attitude is we could if we had to do so.

If it can't potentially be shipped, it's not done. And that is why as agile developers we need to be big on the agile principle and the acceptance of three simple truths.

Agile principle

Working software is the primary measure of success.

1.4 Three Simple Truths

Figure 1, *Three Simple Truths*, on page 10 gives three simple project truths that, once accepted, get rid of much of the drama and dysfunction we regularly see on software projects.

Accepting the first truth means you are not afraid to begin your journey without knowing everything up front. You understand that requirements are meant to be discovered and that not proceeding until all are gathered would mean never starting.

Accepting the second means you no longer fear or avoid change. You know it is coming. You accept it for what it is. You adapt your plan when necessary and move on.

And by accepting the third, you no longer get stressed when your to-do list exceeds your time and resources to deliver. This is the normal state for any

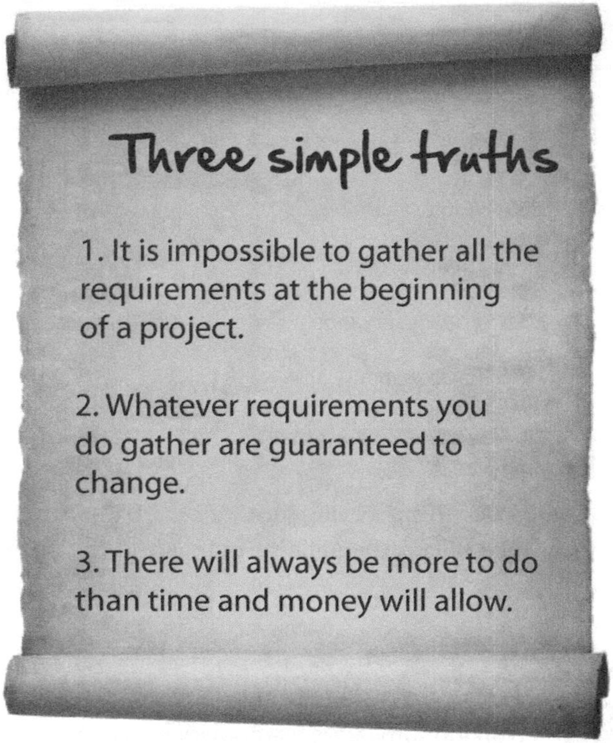

Three simple truths

1. It is impossible to gather all the requirements at the beginning of a project.

2. Whatever requirements you do gather are guaranteed to change.

3. There will always be more to do than time and money will allow.

Figure 1—Three Simple Truths

interesting project. You do the only thing you can—you set some priorities, get the most important stuff done first, and save the least important for last.

Once you accept these three simple project truths, much of the stress and anxiety traditionally associated with software delivery disappears. You are then able to think and innovate with a level of focus and clarity that escapes most in our industry.

And always remember...

There is no one way!

Just like there is no one ultimate flavor of ice cream, there is no one ultimate flavor of agile.

- You've got Scrum—a project management wrapper for managing agile projects.

- You've got XP—the highly disciplined, core software engineering practices essential to every agile project.

- You've got Lean—the ultra-efficient, Toyota Production System equivalent for the ever-improving company.

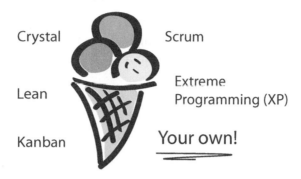

Crystal

Scrum

Lean

Extreme
Programming (XP)

Kanban

Your own!

And then you've got your own agile method—the one you use when you and your family drive halfway across the country only to discover the amusement park you were planning on visiting is closed for renovations.

This book and all the other literature out there on agile are simply shared learnings I and others have found useful when trying to serve customers this way. In this book, I will be sharing with you teachings and innovations from all the agile methods and several we had to invent ourselves. Read them, study them, challenge them, and take from them what you need.

But understand that no book or method can give you everything you'll need, and you can't stop thinking for yourself. Each project is different, and although certain principles and practices will always hold true,[1] how you apply them will depend on your unique situation and context.

A Few Words on Language

Agile terms are pretty consistent across most methodologies, but there are a few terms that differ between the two most popular methods, Extreme Programming and Scrum.

Throughout the book I will try to be consistent (I generally prefer the Extreme Programming terms), but if you hear me say the following, know these terms are interchangeable and are one and the same:

- *Iteration* instead of *sprint*
- *Master story list* instead of *product back log*
- *Customer* instead of *product owner*

---

1.   http://agilemanifesto.org

What's Next?

You've got the basics. Now we are going to shift gears and talk about teams.

In the next chapter on agile teams, we'll discuss what your agile team will look like, what it's like to work on an agile project, and a few things everyone on your team needs to know *before* you start your first agile project.

CHAPTER 2

Meet Your Agile Team

Agile teams are a different beast. On a typical agile project there are no pre-defined roles. Anyone can do anything. And yet among all the chaos, confusion, and lack of formal hierarchy, high-performing agile teams somehow seem to regularly produce quality software.

In this chapter, we are going to take a close look at what makes the agile team tick. We'll look at characteristics of good agile teams, how agile teams are different, and some tips on how to find quality players.

By the end of the chapter, you'll know what a typical agile team looks like, how to form your own, and what they need to know before riding into battle.

2.1 How Are Agile Projects Different?

Before we get into what makes an agile team tick, there are a few things you need to know about agile projects in general.

For one, roles really blur on agile projects. When it's done right, joining an agile team is a lot like working in a mini-startup. People pitch in and do whatever it takes to make the project successful—regardless of title or role.

Yes, people still have core competencies, and, yes, they generally stick to what they are good at. But on an agile project, narrowly defined roles like analyst, programmer, and tester don't really exist—at least not in the traditional sense.

The other thing that's different about an agile team is that analysis, coding, design, and testing are continuous activities—they never end.

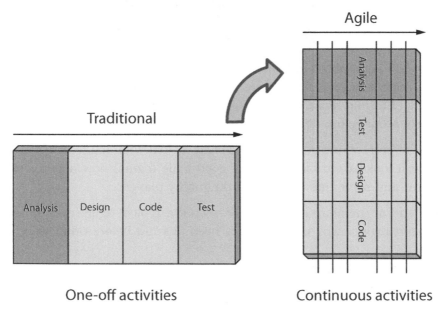

That means these activities can't exist in isolation anymore. The people doing the work need to be joined at the hip working together daily throughout the project.

And the third thing you need to be aware of is just how big agile is on this concept of one team and team accountability.

One team   vs.   Multiple silos

Quality is a team responsibility on an agile project. There is no QA department —you're it, whether you are doing analysis, writing the code, or managing the project. Quality assurance is everywhere, which is why you'll never hear the question "How did QA miss that bug?" on an agile project.

So, blurring roles, continuous development activities, and team accountability are all things you can expect to see on agile teams.

Let's now take a look at some things agile teams do to make themselves successful.

2.2 What Makes an Agile Team Tick

Before you and your team can crush it, there are certain things you're going to want to fight for to help set yourselves up for success.

Co-location

If there was one thing you could do to dramatically improve the productivity of your team, it would be to have everyone sit together.

Co-located teams just work better. Questions get answered fast. Problems are fixed on the spot. There is less friction between interactions. Trust is built more quickly. It's very hard to compete with the power of a small co-located team.

So if co-located teams are so good, does that mean if your team is distributed that you can't run an agile project? Absolutely not.

Distributed teams are becoming a way of life for many. And although a tight co-located team will always have an advantage over a distributed one, there are things you can do to close the gap.

For one, you can reserve some budget at the beginning of your project to bring everyone together. Even if it's just for a few days (even better if you can swing a couple weeks), that time spent getting to know each other, joking around, and eating together goes a long way in turning your ragtag bunch into a tight, high-performing team. So, try to bring everyone together at the start.

After that, you can use every communication tool and trick in the book (Skype, video conferencing, social media tools) to make your distributed team seem like a co-located one even though you're not.

Engaged Customers

There is a lot of software that still gets written today by teams that don't have engaged customers. It's sad, and it ought to be a crime.

How can teams be expected to build compelling, innovative products if the very people they are building them for aren't part of the process?

Engaged customers are those who show up to demos, answer questions, give feedback, and provide the guidance and insight necessary for the team to build compelling software. They are core members of the team and full-on partners during delivery.

That's why agile methods like Extreme Programming and Scrum fight hard for customer engagement through practices like the *on-site customer* and Scrum's dedicated role of *product owner*. It's a big important job. We'll talk more about these roles shortly.

That is also why an engaged customer is necessary for any successful agile project.

Agile principle

Business people and developers must work together daily throughout the project.

Now you may be wondering, "What should I do if I don't have an engaged customer?" Maybe they've been let down in the past, maybe this is a project that they don't think they need, or maybe they just don't think you are going to deliver.

Whatever the issue, if you need to build some customer credibility, do this...

The next time you get in front of your customer, tell them that two weeks from now you are going to make some problem of theirs go away.

Don't ask for permission. Don't make a big ceremony out of it. Just take some problem, or some itch that they have, and make it go away.

Encourage Unplanned Collaborations

In the documentary *The Pixar Touch*, Steve Jobs commented on how dependent Pixar was on unplanned collaborations for the success of its movies. After the release of *Toy Story II* (which just about killed them), he knew they were too spread out, they were too silo'd, and they ran the risk of losing the magic if they didn't do something to bring everyone together.

It was for that reason Pixar acquired 20 acres in Emeryville, California, and brought the whole company together under one roof. The result was instant. Communication improved, collaboration ensued, and they were able to ramp up their production schedule to one major release per year.

Then do it. Come back two weeks later, show them how you've completely solved their problem, and then do it again. Take some other problem, and make it go away.

You may need to do this three or four times (maybe more) before they start to pay much attention, but eventually they will.

They are going to start looking at you differently and see you for what you really are: a fierce executor who can be counted on to get things done.

Look, there could be a thousand reasons why your customer isn't engaged. Maybe they are tired of having projects done to them by the IT department. Maybe they don't want (or need) the software in the first place. Maybe you didn't do a good job setting expectations around how important their role would be to the success of the project. Or maybe they're just really busy.

All I am saying is that if you need to build some credibility, start by making small deposits in the trust bucket, and eventually you'll win them over.

Self-Organizing

Agile teams like to be given a goal and then have everyone stand back as they collectively figure out how to get there. To do that, agile teams need to be able to self-organize.

Self-organization is about checking your ego at the door and working with your team to figure out how you as a team (with all your unique skills, passions, and talents) can best deliver this project.

"Sure, Bobby can cut code. But he also has a great eye for design, so he's going to be helping out with some of the mock-ups."

"Yes, Suzy is one of our best testers, but where she really shines is in setting expectations with the customer. She just has a way, and she loves doing it."

This doesn't mean developers need to be experts in visual design or testers are now expected to handle the project management.

It's more an acknowledgment that the best way to build teams is to let the role fit the person, instead of making the person fit the role.

So, how do you get your team to self-organize?

- You let them create the plan, come up with the estimates, and take ownership of the project.

- You worry less about titles and roles and become more interested in seeing the continuous production of working, tested software.

- You look for people who can take initiative, like being the masters of their own destiny, and don't sit back and wait for orders.

In short, you let the reins go and trust and empower them to get the job done.

Agile principle

The best architectures, requirements, and designs emerge from self-organizing teams.

Now, self-organization by itself is great, but the real magic kicks in because of what that leads to—empowerment and accountability.

Accountable and Empowered

A good agile team will always want to be held accountable for the results they produce. They know customers are counting on them to come through, and they won't shirk from the responsibility that comes with having to deliver value from day one.

Of course, being accountable works only if teams are truly empowered. Giving your team the reins to make their own decisions and do what they think is right frees them to take initiative and act on their own accord. They solve their own problems, and they don't wait for anyone to give them permission.

Sure, you'll make an occasional mistake. But the upside is so big that it's worth the risk.

Agile principle

Build projects around motivated individuals.
Give them the environment and support they need,
and trust them to get the job done.

Now, creating an empowered and accountable team is easier said than done —not everyone wants to be empowered. Why bother when it's so much easier just to show up, chop the vegetables, and do what you're told?

If you think you have an issue with accountability, there is an easy fix—get your team to demo their software.

The simple act of putting teams in front of real live customers and having them demo their software will go miles toward making your team more accountable.

First, your team will see that real people are counting on them to deliver. They will realize there are real people, with real problems, who need real software to make their lives better.

Second, it will take only one bad demo for your team to take a sudden interest in making sure the software is ready for feedback and everything works. They will insist on becoming empowered to make this happen. If they don't, you have a bigger problem.

Cross-Functional

A cross-functional team is one that can serve their customer from end to end. That means having the necessary skills and expertise on your team to take any feature your customer would need and be able to deliver it fully.

When recruiting people for your team, you'll want generalists, people who are comfortable doing a wide variety of things. For programmers, that means finding people who are comfortable walking the entire technology stack (not just the front end or back end). For testers and analysts, that means people who are just as comfortable testing as they are doing a deep-dive analysis on the requirements.

Specialists are used on occasion when the team lacks some sort of specific skill (such as database tuning). But mostly the team sticks together and works together as one for the duration of the project.

Of course, the real beauty of the cross-functional team is the speed at which they can go. Without having to wait for permission or negotiate for resources from others, they can start delivering value from day one, with no one in their way to stop them.

OK, so those are some expectations you're going to want to set and some things you're going to want to fight for when forming your team.

Now let's take a look at some roles.

2.3   Roles We Typically See

Agile methods like Scrum and XP don't have a lot of formal roles when it comes to projects. There are people who know what needs to be built (customers) and people who can build it (the development team).

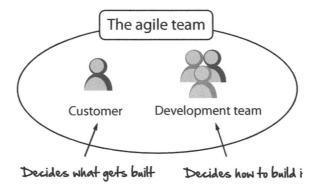

Now if you are wondering where all the programmers, testers, and analysts are, don't worry—they're still there. Agile is just less concerned about who plays what role and more worried about the right roles being played.

Let's start though by taking a look at one of the most important roles on any agile project: the agile customer.

Who Moved My Cheese?

Who Moved My Cheese? [Joh98] is a business fable about mice who wake up one day to discover that the big block of cheese they have built a comfortable life around is gone. Someone has moved it. And now they are at a loss as to what to do.

For some, transitioning to agile can feel a bit like someone has moved their cheese.

For the project manager, it can be the realization that no matter how hard they try, the requirements are going to change.

For the analyst, it's the realization that analysis on an agile project never ends.

For the developer, it's the expectation that they will be expected to write tests (and lots of them!).

So, understand that when you are changing how people work, you are moving someone's cheese. And anything you can do to help them find the new cheese (such as showing them how their roles will change) will help.

The Agile Customer

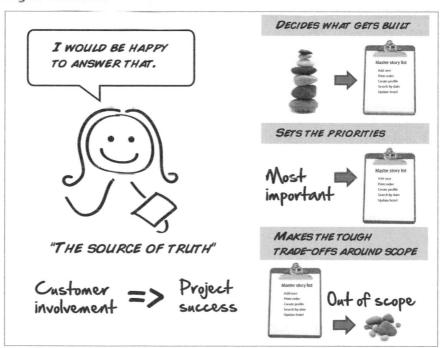

The agile customer is the "source of the truth" from which all requirements flow on an agile project. They are the people for whom the software is being built.

Ideally they would be a subject-matter expert. It's someone intimately familiar with the business, who really cares what the software does, what it looks like, and how it works, and who is committed to guiding the team, answering questions, and giving feedback.

They also set the priorities. They decide what gets built and when.

This isn't done in a vacuum. It's a collaborative process with the development team because there may be technical reasons why it makes more sense to work on some features before others (in other words, to reduce technical risk).

But generally they set the priorities from a business point of view, and then they work with the development team to come up with a plan to make it happen.

And they have the fun job of deciding what not to build as deadlines approach and time and money start to run out.

Of course, to do all these things, it helps if the customer is working very closely with the development team—ideally full-time. In early versions of XP, this is referred to as the *on-site customer*, and in Scrum it is known as the full-time role of *product owner*.

Now don't panic if you don't have or can't get a full-time customer—few teams can. You can still do agile and still have a very successful project. Not all projects need or require a full-time customer.

What's more important is to understand the spirit of where agile methods like XP and Scrum are coming from, which is that the more direct involvement you have with your customer, the better.

So, get as much customer involvement as you can, make sure they understand the importance of their role, and make sure they are empowered and willing to make the kinds of decisions that need to be made for the success of the project.

Let's now take a look at the development team.

The Development Team

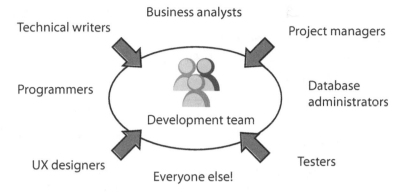

The agile development team is a cross-functional group of people who can take any feature the customer would like developed and turn it into production-ready, working software. This includes analysts, developers, testers, database administrators (DBAs), and anyone else required to turn user stories into working software.

Now, as much I as like the spirit and intent behind the no-formal-role agile team, taking a deeply traditional software team and suddenly telling them they need to "self-organize" has never really worked for me in practice.

To be sure, you can't mince words and need to make it crystal clear that roles blur on agile projects and they are going to be expected to wear many hats. But I've had more success transitioning teams when I present agile in terms and words they already know and understand.

If your team falls into this category, here are some agile role descriptions to help your team make the transition and explain how their roles change on an agile project.

The Agile Analyst

When a feature comes up for development, someone has to get in there and figure out all the nitty-gritty details of how it needs to work. That's our agile analyst.

The analyst is the relentless detective who asks the deep probing questions and gets a thrill from working closely with the customer to really understand what they need of their software.

Analysts do lots of things on agile projects. They help customers write user stories (Chapter 6, *Gathering User Stories*, on page 79). They do the deep dive on the analysis when a story comes up for development. And they can help create mock-ups, create prototypes, and use everything in their analysis toolkit to help communicate the essence of the story.

We'll talk more about how agile analysis works in Section 9.4, *Step 1: Analysis and Design: Making the Work Ready*, on page 147.

The Agile Programmer

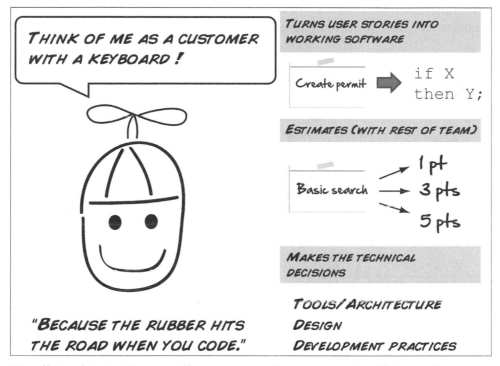

It's all good intentions until someone writes some code. This is where our agile programmers come in.

Agile programmers are pros because they take things like software quality very seriously. The best are passionate testers who take pride in their work and are always looking for an edge in writing higher-quality code.

To that end, there are certain things agile programmers do when regularly creating high-quality, production-ready software.

- They write lots of tests and will often use tests as a means of driving out their designs (Chapter 12, *Unit Testing: Knowing It Works*, on page 185, and Chapter 14, *Test-Driven Development*, on page 207).

- They are continuously designing and improving the architecture of their software as they go (Chapter 13, *Refactoring: Paying Down Your Technical Debt*, on page 195).

- They make sure the code base is always in a state of production readiness and ready to deploy at a moment's notice (Chapter 15, *Continuous Integration: Making It Production-Ready*, on page 217).

And they work very closely with the customer, and everyone else on the team, to ensure that what gets built works, that it is as simple as possible, and that pushing software live into production is a nonevent.

The Agile Tester

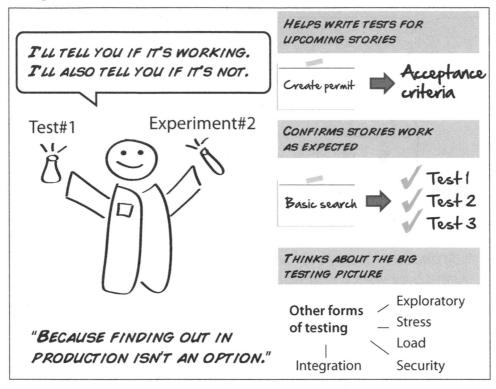

Agile testers know that although it's one thing to build it, it is another to know it works. For that reason, the agile tester will insert themselves into the agile project early, ensuring that success for user stories gets defined up front and that when working software is produced, it works.

Because everything on an agile project needs to be tested, you will find the agile tester everywhere.

You'll find them working side-by-side with the customer helping them capture their requirements in the form of tests.

You'll find them working closely with developers, helping with test automation, looking for holes, and doing extensive exploratory testing by trying to break the application from all possible angles.

They will also have in mind the big testing picture and never lose sight of load testing, scalability, and anything else the team could be doing to produce high-quality software.

Janet Gregory and Lisa Crispin's book *Agile Testing: A Practical Guide for Testers and Agile Teams [CG08]* is a good reference for more about the important role of agile testing.

We talk more about the mechanics of agile testing in Section 9.6, *Step 3: Test: Check the Work*, on page 154.

The Agile Project Manager

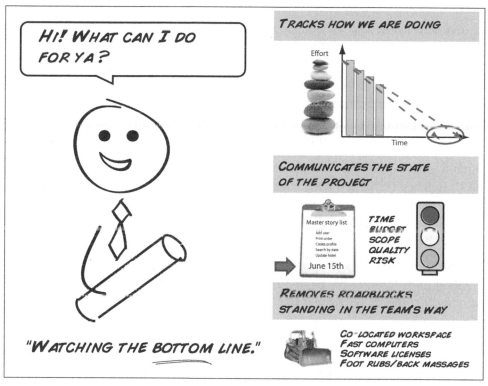

The agile project manager (PM) knows that the only way they'll be successful is if the team is successful. That is why a good PM will go to the ends of the earth to remove anything standing in the way of their team and success. Part of this means continuously planning, replanning, and adjusting course when necessary (Chapter 8, *Agile Planning: Dealing with Reality*, on page 113).

It also means setting expectations upward and outward to the greater project community: getting status reports to stakeholders, forging relationships

> ## What If You Started Every Project Off Like This?
>
> Imagine if you started every project by sharing the answers to four simple questions about yourself with the team:
>
> - What am I good at?
> - How do I perform?
> - What do I value?
> - What results can you expect me to deliver?
>
> Then with this newfound insight, what if you asked them to answer the same questions and to tell you what they were good at, how they performed, what they valued, and the results they could be expected to deliver on the project?
>
> This is the idea behind what I call the Drucker Exercise.[a] It's a simple yet powerful team-building exercise for forming the necessary communication and trust patterns essential to any high-performing team.
>
> _____
>
> a.   http://agilewarrior.wordpress.com/2009/11/27/the-drucker-exercise

within the company, and shielding the team from outside forces when necessary. It's all the good stuff PMs normally do.

A good agile PM doesn't tell the team what to do, though—they don't have to do that. They've helped create an environment such that the team is mostly independent and would continue to deliver fine in the PM's absence. In fact, the hallmark of a good agile PM is the ability to disappear for a week and no one be the wiser.

We talk more about agile project management in Chapter 8, *Agile Planning: Dealing with Reality*, on page 113 and in Chapter 9, *Iteration Management: Making It Happen*, on page 143.

The Agile UX Designer

User experience designers are deeply focused on creating useful, usable, desirable experiences for the customer. Someone passionate about usability would be deeply interested in understanding what the customer needs and then collaborating with the rest of the team to figure out how best to meet them.

Fortunately, many of the practices used by usability experts dovetail nicely with the spirit of agile software delivery. Focusing on value, rapid feedback, and building the best product you can for your customer is something both the UX and agile communities have in common.

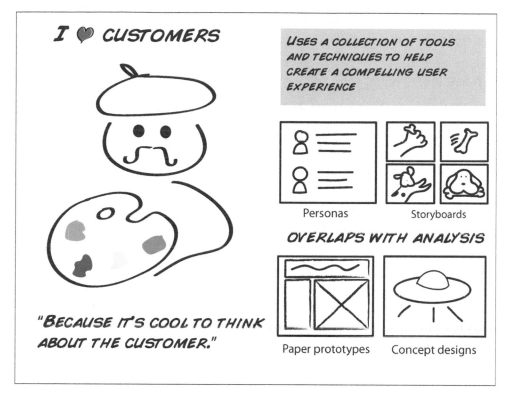

I ♥ CUSTOMERS

USES A COLLECTION OF TOOLS AND TECHNIQUES TO HELP CREATE A COMPELLING USER EXPERIENCE

Personas   Storyboards

OVERLAPS WITH ANALYSIS

"BECAUSE IT'S COOL TO THINK ABOUT THE CUSTOMER."

Paper prototypes   Concept designs

As well, UX designers aren't afraid to design incrementally and iteratively. They will build and design features as the code gets written (instead of trying to design everything up front and getting miles ahead of everyone else).

If you have the luxury of getting someone steeped in usability on your project, consider yourself lucky. They can bring a lot of useful experience and knowledge to the project and really help out in the area of analysis and user experience design.

Everyone Else

And then there's all the other important roles and people we didn't mention: database administrators (DBAs), system administrators (SAs), technical writers, trainers, business improvement, infrastructure, and networking. They are all part of the development team and treated just like anyone else on the project.

Scrum has a role called *scrum master*, which is kind of like an agile coach and rock-star project manager all rolled up in one. Agile coaches can be very helpful in getting new teams going. They can help explain and promote the agile principles and philosophies, and they can ensure teams stay the course and don't slip back into old bad habits. For a good book on coaching, check out *Agile Coaching [SD09]*.

Experienced teams typically don't need dedicated coaches, but new projects can definitely benefit from having them around.

One final thing: when you present these roles, make sure people understand that it's OK (and expected) for people to wear multiple hats on an agile project.

In other words, let your analysts know that it's OK for developers to talk directly to the customer (in fact, it's encouraged). Let your testers know that developers are going to be expected to write a lot of automated tests. And just because your project doesn't have a dedicated UX designer doesn't mean usability and design don't get done. They do—just by someone else wearing that hat on the team.

Let's wrap up by going over some things to look for when recruiting players for your team.

2.4 Tips for Forming Your Agile Team

Although most people would enjoy working on any high-performing agile team, there are some things to look for when finding quality players.

Look for Generalists

Generalists do well on agile projects because agile requires people to follow through and own opportunities from end to end. For programmers, that means coders who can walk the entire stack (front end to back). For analysts and testers, that means being comfortable doing analysis and testing.

Generalists are also comfortable wearing many hats. They might be coding one day, doing analysis the next, and testing after that.

People Who Are Comfortable with Ambiguity

Not everything is going to be neat and tidy on an agile project. The requirements won't all be there—you're going to need to discover them. The plan is going to change, and you are going to have to adapt and change with it.

Look for people who don't panic when curve balls are thrown at them, who can take a punch, and who can deal with the change train as it comes rolling down the track.

Team Players Who Can Check Their Egos at the Door

It sounds like a cliche, but agile works best with folks who can act as an ensemble and check their egos at the door.

Not everyone likes the role blurring agile brings. Some people get protective over what they see as "their" turf.

Just look for people who are comfortable in their own skins, aren't afraid to share, and sincerely enjoy learning and growing with others.

Master Sensei and the aspiring warrior

STUDENT: *Master, I am confused. If there are no predefined roles on agile project, how does anything ever get done?*

MASTER: *That which needs to be done, the team will do.*

STUDENT: *Yes, Master, but if there is no dedicated role of tester, how can we be sure that enough testing will be done?*

MASTER: *Testing is something that needs to be done. So, testing is something the team will do. How much testing and in what capacity is up to the team to decide.*

STUDENT: *What if no one wants to test? What if everyone just wants to sit around and write code?*

MASTER: *Then you'd best find people who have a passion for testing and make sure they become valued members of your team.*

STUDENT: *Thank you, Master. I will think about this more.*

What's Next?

You now see how roles blur on agile projects, why we would ideally like our teams to be co-located, and how, when finding people for your team, you are going to want generalists and people who are cool with dealing with ambiguity.

You are now ready for what is perhaps one of the most important steps in kick-starting your agile project (and an area that most agile methods are completely silent on)—agile project inception.

Turn the page, to Part II of the book, and find out how to set your project up for success from the start and make sure you have the right people.

Part II

Agile Project Inception

CHAPTER 3

How to Get Everyone on the Bus

Many projects get killed before they even get out of the starting blocks. This is mostly because of the following reasons:

- They fail to ask the right questions.
- They don't have the courage to ask the tough ones.

In this part, we are going to look at a powerful expectation-setting tool called the *inception deck*—ten questions you'd be crazy not to ask before starting any software project. By harnessing the power of the inception deck, you'll make sure you get the right people on your bus and that it's headed in the right direction long before the first line of code ever gets written.

3.1 What Kills Most Projects

At the start of any new project, people usually have wildly different ideas about what success looks like.

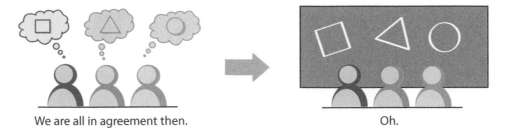

We are all in agreement then.   Oh.

This can be deadly for projects because although we will all be using the same words and phrases to describe what we want, it's only when we start delivering that we realize we're all thinking completely different things.

And the problem isn't that we aren't all aligned at the start (that's natural). It's that we start our projects *before* everyone is on board.

The assumption of consensus where none exists is what kills most projects.

What we need is something that does the following:

- Communicates the goals, vision, and context of the project to the team so they can make intelligent decisions while executing

- Gives the stakeholders the information they need to help them make that go/no-go decision on whether or not to proceed with the project

What if we did this ...   Ah!

And the only way to get this is to ask the tough questions.

3.2   Ask the Tough Questions

Working Down Under, I had the opportunity to ride shotgun with one of ThoughtWorks' top professional services salespeople—a gentleman by the name of Keith Dodds. One of the many things Keith taught me was the importance of asking the tough questions at the start of any new engagement or sale.

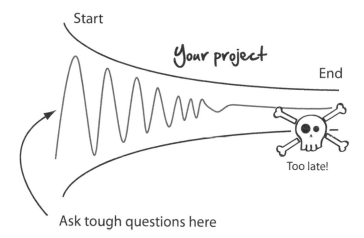

Start

Your project

End

Too late!

Ask tough questions here

You see, in the beginning of any new engagement or project, you have a lot of leeway in the questions you can ask with little to lose. You can ask wide-open questions like the following:

- How much experience does your team have?
- Have you ever done this type of thing before?
- How much money do we have?
- Who's calling the shots on this project?
- Do you see any challenges with having two analysts and thirty developers?
- Which other projects have you worked on where you were able to take a team of junior developers with little or no object-oriented experience and successfully rewrite a legacy mainframe system in Ruby on Rails using agile?

You want to take the same approach when kicking off your agile project. You want to ask all the scary questions up front. And one tool for helping you do that is the inception deck.

3.3 Enter the Inception Deck

The inception deck (Figure 2, *The Inception Deck*, on page 38) is your flashlight for dispelling the mist and mystery around your agile project. It's a collection of ten tough questions and exercises you'd be crazy not to do and ask before starting any project.

We used it often at ThoughtWorks to cover an area of project initiation that agile methods like Extreme Programming (XP) and Scrum were silent on—project chartering. We knew heavy six-month analysis and requirements-gathering exercises weren't the way to go, but we didn't have any lightweight

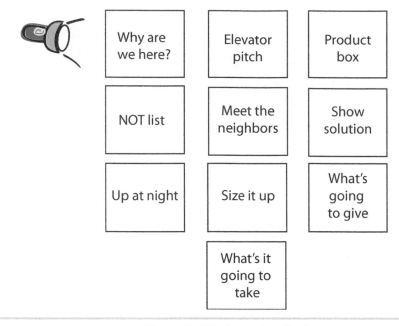

Why are we here?	Elevator pitch	Product box
NOT list	Meet the neighbors	Show solution
Up at night	Size it up	What's going to give
	What's it going to take	

Figure 2—The Inception Deck

alternatives. It was in this spirit that Robin Gibbons created the original inception deck: a fast, lightweight way to distill a project to its very core and communicate that shared understanding to the greater team and community.

3.4 How It Works

The idea behind the inception deck is that if we can get the right people in the room and ask them the right questions, this will do wonders for collectively setting expectations about our project.

By putting the team through a series of exercises and capturing the output on a slide deck (usually PowerPoint), we can collectively get a pretty good idea about what this project is, what it isn't, and what it's going to take to deliver.

The right people for the inception deck are anyone directly involved in the project. This includes customers, stakeholders, team members, developers, testers, analysts—anyone who can materially contribute to the effective execution of the project.

It is also really important that you get the stakeholders involved, because the inception deck is not only a tool for us but also for them to help make that critical go/no-go decision on whether we should even proceed.

A typical inception deck can take anywhere from a couple days to about two weeks to build. It's good for about six months of project planning and should be revisited anytime there is a major change in the spirit or direction of the project.

That's because the inception deck is a living, breathing artifact. It's not something we do once and then file away. Upon completion, teams like to put it up on the wall in their work areas to let it serve as a reminder about what they are working on and why.

And of course, the questions and exercises presented here are just the beginning. You are going to think of other questions, exercises, and things you are going to want to clarify before you start.

So, use this as a starting point, but don't follow it blindly or be afraid to change it up to make it your own.

3.5 The Inception Deck in a Nutshell

Here's a high-level overview of the inception deck questions and exercises:

1. Ask why we are here.

   - This is a quick reminder about why we are here, who our customers are, and why we decided to do this project in the first place.

2. Create an elevator pitch.

   - If we had thirty seconds and two sentences to describe our project, what would we say?

3. Design a product box.

   - If we were flipping through a magazine and we saw an advertisement for our product or service, what would it say, and, more importantly, would we buy it?

4. Create a NOT list.

   - It's pretty clear what we want to do on this project. Let's be even clearer and show what we are not doing.

5. Meet your neighbors.

   - Our project community is always bigger than we think. Why don't we invite them over for coffee and introduce ourselves?

6. Show the solution.

- Let's draw the high-level blueprints of the technical architecture to make sure we are all thinking of the same thing.

7. Ask what keeps us up at night.

   - Some of the things that happen on projects are downright scary. But talking about them, and what we can do to avoid them, can make them less scary.

8. Size it up.

   - Is this thing a three-, six-, or nine-month project?

9. Be clear on what's going to give.

   - Projects have levers like time, scope, budget, and quality. What's most and least important for this project at this time?

10. Show what it's going to take.

    - How long is it going to take? How much will it cost? And what kind of team are we going to need to pull this off?

We'll cover the inception deck in two parts. In Chapter 4, *Seeing the Big Picture*, on page 41, we'll go over the *why* behind the project, while in Chapter 5, *Making It Real*, on page 57 we'll go over the *how*.

Let's start with the why.

Seeing the Big Picture

Software is one of those unique activities that combines design, construction, art, and science all rolled up into one. Teams face thousands of decisions and trade-offs every day. And without the right context or big-picture understanding, it's impossible for them to make the right trade-offs in an informed or balanced way.

In the first half of the inception deck, we are going to get really clear on the *why* behind our project by answering questions like the following:

- Why are we here?
- What's our elevator pitch?
- What would an ad for our product look like?
- What are we not going to do?
- Who's in our neighborhood?

By the end of this chapter, you and your team will have a clear understanding of what the goal of the project is, will know why you are building it, and will be able to communicate clearly and quickly to others.

But let's first start by asking our sponsors why we are here.

4.1   Ask: Why Are We Here?

Before any project team can be really successful, they need to understand the *why* behind what they are building. When they understand the *why*, teams can do the following:

- Make better, more informed decisions
- Do a better job of balancing the conflicting forces and trade-offs
- Come up with better, more innovative solutions because they are empowered to think for themselves

It's all about discovering your *commander's intent* and *going and seeing* for yourself.

Go and See for Yourself

It's one thing to intellectually understand why we're here. It's something else entirely to know it. To really get inside your customers' heads and really understand what they need, you must go and see for yourself.

Going and seeing is about getting your team off their butts and out into the field where the action is.

For example, if you are building a permit system for a construction company out at the mine site, go to the construction site. Hang with the safety officers. See the trailers. Observe the cramped conditions, flaky Internet connections, and confined spaces your customers work in. Spend a day at the site, and work with the people who are going to be using your system day in and day out.

Get engaged, ask questions, and become your customer.

Toyota: The Masters of Go and See

In his excellent book *The Toyota Way [Lik04]*, Jeffrey Liker describes the story of how the chief engineer charged with redesigning the 2004 Toyota Sienna wanted to improve the design for North Americans. To get a feel for how North Americans lived, worked, and played with their vehicles, he and his team drove a Toyota Sienna through every U.S. state and its provinces, Canada, and Mexico.

What he discovered was the following:

- North American drivers eat and drink more in their cars than drivers do in Japan (where driving distances are typically shorter). For that reason, you will find a center tray and fourteen cup holders standard in every Toyota Sienna.

- Roads in Canada have a higher crown than in America (bowed up in the middle), so controlling the "drift" while driving was very important.

- Severe cross winds in Ontario made side-wind stability a much bigger issue to be dealt with. If you drive any place with a strong cross wind, the new Sienna is much more stable and easier to handle.

While the chief engineer might have been able to read about these issues in a marketing report, he would not have gained the new level of appreciation and understanding he now has by going and seeing these things for himself.

Discover Your Commander's Intent

Commander's intent is a concise expression, phrase, or statement that summarizes the goal or purpose of your project or mission. It's that statement, or guiding light, you can turn to in the 11th hour, in the thick of the battle, that helps you decide whether to press the attack or hold your ground.

In *Made to stick [HH07]*, Chip and Dan Heath describe a story where Southwest Airlines was debating whether to add a Caesar chicken salad to one of its flights.

When asked if it would lower the cost of the price of the ticket (CEO Herbs Kelleher's commander's intent), it became clear that adding the option of a chicken salad didn't make sense.

The commander's intent for your project doesn't have to be something big or aspirational. It can be something really simple and focused for your project.

The key to this exercise is to get people talking about why they *think* they are here and then validate with your customer whether that's really what it's all about.

There Are a Dozen Reasons for Doing Your Project

I recently did this exercise with a team charged with creating invoices for a new division of the company and was amazed by the variety of reasons why the team thought they were there.

Some thought it was to reduce the number of pages on the invoice to save paper. Others thought it was to simplify the invoice and thus reduce call center volume. Still others thought it was an opportunity to run targeted marketing campaigns in an attempt to up-sell customers on products and services.

All were good answers, and any of them would have warranted a project in their own right. But it was only through much discussion, debate, and understanding that the true goal of the project emerged—which was to simplify the invoice and reduce call center volume.

4.2 Create an Elevator Pitch

The Elevator Pitch

- **For** [construction managers]
- **who** [need to track what type of work is being done on the construction site],
- **the** [CSWP*]
- **is a** [safety work permit system],
- **that** [creates, tracks, and audits safety work permits].
- **Unlike** [the current paper-based system]
- **our product** [is web based and can be accessed any time from anywhere].

*CSWP: Construction Safety Work Permit

Quick! The venture capitalist (VC) you have been trying to get in front of for the last three months just walked into the elevator, and you have thirty seconds to pitch the idea for your new fledgling start-up. Success means fuel for your venture. Failure means more Kraft dinner.

That's the idea behind the elevator pitch—a way of communicating the essence of your idea in a very short period of time. Elevator pitches aren't just for aspiring entrepreneurs, though. They are also great for concisely defining new software projects.

A good elevator pitch will do a number of things for your project.

1. It brings clarity.

   Instead of trying to be all things to all people, the elevator pitch forces teams to answer tough questions about what the product is and who it's for.

2. It forces teams to think about the customer.

   By bringing focus into what the product does and why, teams gain valuable insight into what's compelling about the product and why their customers are buying it in the first place.

3. It gets to the point.

   Like a laser, the elevator pitch cuts through a lot of cruft and gets to the heart of what the project is about. This clarity helps set priorities and greatly increases the signal-to-noise ratio of what really matters.

Let's now look at a template to help form your pitch.

The Elevator Pitch Template

- For [target customer]
- who [statement of need or opportunity]
- the [product name]
- is a [product category]
- that [key benefit, compelling reason to buy].
- Unlike [primary competitive alternative]
- our product [statement of primary differentiation].

Being Brief Is Tough

One of the reasons the elevator pitch is so powerful is because it is short. But don't be fooled into thinking that writing something short is easy.

It may take you and your team a couple tries before you get a good pitch, so don't worry if you don't nail it the first time. Writing a good elevator pitch can be hard work —but so worth it.

I would have written you a shorter letter, but I didn't have the time. —derived from Blaise Pascal, Provincial Letters XVI

There's no one way to do an elevator pitch. The one I like comes from Geoffrey Moore's book *Crossing the Chasm [Moo91]*.

- *For* [target customer]—Explains who the project is for or who would benefit from its usage.

- *who* [statement of need or opportunity]—Expands on the problem or need the customer has to solve.

- *the* [product name]—Gives life to our project by giving it a name. Names are important because they communicate intent.

- *is a* [product category]—Explains what this service or product actually is or does.

- *that* [key benefit, compelling reason to buy]—Explains why our customer would want to buy this product in the first place.

- *Unlike* [primary competitive alternative]—Covers why we wouldn't already use what's out there.

- *our product* [statement of primary differentiation]—Differentiate and explains how our service is different or better than the competing alternatives. This is the big one. It is where we are really justifying the expenditure of money on our project.

- The two sentences of the elevator pitch beautifully capture everything we need to quickly communicate the essence of our project or idea. They tell us what our product is, who it's for, and why anyone would want to buy it in the first place.

There are a couple of ways you can do the elevator pitch with your team. You can print the template and have everyone take a stab at filling it out themselves before bringing everyone together.

Or, if you want to save a few trees, you can just beam the template up onto the screen and tackle filling it out as a group, going through each element of the template one section at a time.

With your elevator pitch in hand, let's now turn on your creative juices and design a box for your product.

4.3 Design a Product Box

The Construction
Safety Permit System

Ideal for mine sites

Process permits faster!
Process permits safer!
Track people's time better!

Where you need it. When you need it.

Software is sometimes a necessary evil for companies. Rather than take on all the risk and uncertainty that comes with large projects, many would rather walk into their local Wal-Mart, whip out the credit card, and simply buy whatever it is they need.

While shrink-wrapped million-dollar software packages on supermarket shelves might still be a long way off, it does raise an interesting question. If we could buy our software off the supermarket shelf, what would the product box look like? And more importantly, would we buy it?

Creating a product box for your project, and asking why someone would buy it, gets your team focused on what's compelling for your customer and the underlying benefits of your product. Both are good things for teams to be aware of while delivering.

How Does It Work?

Now, I know what you're thinking. "I'm not creative. I'm not in advertising. I couldn't possibly create an ad for my product."

Well, I've got news for you. You absolutely can. And I am going to show you how in three easy steps.

Step 1: Brainstorm Your Product's Benefits

Never tell your customers about your product's features—they won't care. What people are interested in, however, is how your product is going to make their lives easier, in other words, your product's benefits.

For example, say we were trying to convince a family on the merits of purchasing a mini-van. We could show them a list of all the features. Or we could show them the benefits of how the mini-van would make their lives better.

Features Benefits

Features	Benefits
245 horsepower engine	Pass easy on the highway
Cruise control	Save money
Anti-lock brakes	Brake safely with loved ones

Be sure to convert any features into benefits!

See the difference?

So, step 1 in creating your product box is to sit down with your team and customer and brainstorm all the reasons why people would want to use your product. Then pick your top three.

Step 2: Create a Slogan

The key to any good slogan is to say as much as possible in very few words. I don't have to tell you what these companies stand for because their slogans say it all:

- Acura—The true definition of luxury. Yours.
- FedEx—Peace of mind.
- Starbucks—Rewarding everyday moments.

Did you feel the emotion that came from these slogans?

Now relax. These are some pretty sweet slogans, and yours doesn't have to be quite so pro. Just get together with your team, brainstorm your slogan in a time-box of ten or fifteen minutes, and have some fun exercising that creative part of your brain. Remember, no slogan is too cheesy.

Step 3: Design the Box

Excellent! You are almost there. With your three compelling reasons to buy and your irresistible catchy slogan, you are now ready to bring it together.

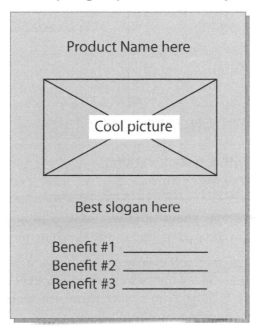

For this exercise, imagine your customer walked into your local software store and saw your product box sitting there on the shelf. And when they picked it up, it looked so compelling that they instantly bought ten copies for themselves and their friends.

Now quick, draw that box!

Don't worry about creating the *Mona Lisa*. Just use flip chart paper, colored markers, papers, stickies, and whatever you can get your hands on. Shout out your slogan. Show your customers the benefits. Spend fifteen minutes designing the best product box you can.

Excellent! See, that wasn't so hard. Have some fun with this exercise (it's not every day you get to use crayons and draw compelling product pictures). It's a great team builder and a fun way to think critically about the *why* behind your software.

Now let's see what we can do to start setting expectations around the scope of your project.

4.4   Create a NOT List

IN SCOPE	OUT OF SCOPE

Create new permit
Update/Read/Delete
    existing permits
Search
Basic reporting
Print
	Interfacing with legacy
	    road closure system
	Offline capability

UNRESOLVED
Integration with logistics tracking Security card swipe system

When setting expectations about the scope of your project, saying what you are *not* going to do can be just as important as what you are.

By creating a NOT list, you will clearly state what is in and out of scope for your project. Doing this will not only set clear expectations with your customer, but will also ensure that you and your team are focusing on the really important stuff while ignoring everything else.

How Does It Work?

IN	OUT
Big rocks we need to move	Stuff we aren't going to sweat

UNRESOLVED
Things we still need to sort out

The Million-Dollar Question

I was once doing an inception deck with a large Canadian utility when the VP of the division asked how this new system was going to integrate with the existing legacy mainframe.

You could have heard a pin drop in the room. The VP, the one signing the checks and ultimately responsible for the success of this project, didn't understand that the new system was never going to integrate with the old one. It was going to replace it entirely.

It was only because we threw up the NOT list that we avoided a major expectation reset at some later point in the project. It's better to do it now than try to reset something like that when the project is already underway.

The NOT list is a great visual for clearly showing what's in and out of scope for your project. Basically, you get together with your customer and team and fill in the blanks brainstorming all the high-level features they'd like to see in their software.

IN contains the stuff we want to focus on. Here we are saying, "These are the big rocks we are going to be moving on this project." They can be high-level features (that is, reporting), or they could be general objectives (that is, Amazon-like scalability).

OUT contains the stuff that we aren't going to sweat. It might be stuff we are going to defer to the next release, or it's simply beyond the scope of this project. But for now, we aren't going to worry about it. It's off the table.

UNRESOLVED lists the things we still need to make a decision about. This is a great section because it reflects the reality about most software projects. They could be many things to many people—which is exactly what we want to avoid. Eventually, we would like to move all our UNRESOLVED to the IN or OUT sections.

The beauty of this visual is how much it communicates at a glance. By listing the big ticket items in scope on the left, out of scope on the right, and then unresolved on the bottom, everyone can get a clear picture at a glance of where the boundaries of our project lie.

With our scope clearly defined, let's now move on and see who's in our project neighborhood.

4.5 Meet Your Neighbors

Good neighbors can be your best friends. They are there when you lock yourself out of the house. They are there when you need that power tool. And it feels pretty darn good when you help them set up that wireless home network.

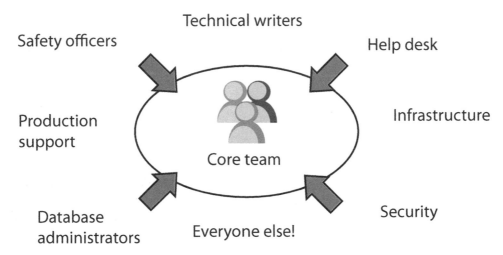

Believe it or not, you have neighbors on your projects too. Only instead of keeping a spare key and lending you power tools, they manage databases, do security audits, and keep your networks running.

By meeting your neighbors, you can build relationships up front that will give big dividends down the road. It's also courteous to say "hi" instead of just running to them when your house is on fire. And most important, it's essential for building the foundation of every successful project community—trust.

My First Big Project Blunder

We all make mistakes. One of my biggest was as a team lead at ThoughtWorks while we were doing some work at Microsoft.

I went in there and started executing the project thinking our project community looked something like this:

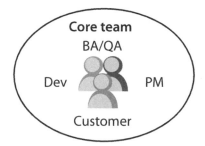

And for a while everything was fine. The team was doing agile. We were regularly delivering working software, and life was good.

Then near the end of the project something strange started to happen. Groups and people I had never seen or met suddenly started coming out of nowhere and making ridiculous demands of me and the team.

- One group wanted to review our architecture (as if our architecture needed reviewing!).

- Another wanted to make sure we were complying with corporate security policies (bah!).

- And another wanted to review our documentation (what documentation!).

Who were these people? Where did they come from? And why were they so intent on messing up our schedule?

Overnight, our nice little project community went from a small team of six to something much bigger and vast.

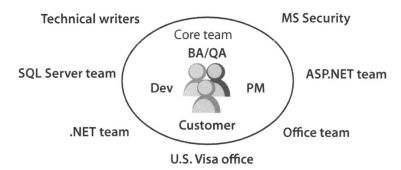

While I felt like blaming others for impacts to our schedule, the reality was I didn't appreciate that *your project community is always bigger than you think.*[1]

---

1. *The Blind Men and the Elephant [Sch03]*

Coffee, Donuts, and Sincerity

When it comes to building respectful relationships with neighbors, it's hard to beat a good cup of coffee and a sweet-tasting donut...

Coffee because it comes served in a nice warm vessel, and as they're enjoying it, they will associate you with feelings of warmth.

Donuts because as you are telling your neighbor how much you appreciate having them around, their bodies will be rejoicing with the taste of pure sugar, and so they will associate you with sweetness.

But the ultimate tool for great relationships with your neighbors is sincerity.

To truly make your neighbors feel appreciated and valued, you gotta mean it. They will see through insincere flattery in an instant. But genuine appreciation and sincere thanks will go miles to winning them over. And you and your project will prosper more for it.

With "Meet the neighbors," you want to map out who is in your project community, get them on your radar, and start building relationships before you need them. That way, when the time comes, you won't be complete strangers, and they'll be in a much better position to help you.

How Does It Work?

With your team, get together and brainstorm everyone you think you are going to need to interact with before your project can go live. Team members who have been with the company a long time and are aware of all the corporate policies and organizational hoops will be invaluable here.

Greater community

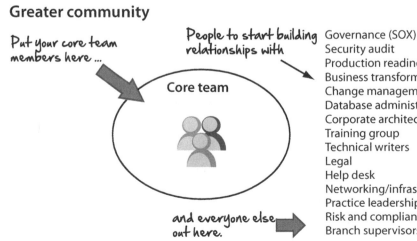

Put your core team members here ...

People to start building relationships with

Core team

and everyone else out here.

Governance (SOX)
Security audit
Production readiness
Business transformation
Change management
Database administrators
Corporate architecture
Training group
Technical writers
Legal
Help desk
Networking/infrastructure
Practice leadership team
Risk and compliance
Branch supervisors

Then once you've gotten the lay of the land, talk about each group and see whether you can start assigning contact names. Your project manager, or whomever on the team is going to take lead on building these external project relationships, can then come up with a game plan of engaging these groups.

Master Sensei and the aspiring warrior

STUDENT: *Master, many of these exercises require time from your sponsors and stakeholders. What if they are unavailable or are just too busy to answer these types of questions about the project?*

MASTER: *Then you should congratulate yourself. For you have just discovered your first major project risk.*

STUDENT: *What risk is that?*

MASTER: *Customer engagement. Without an engaged customer, your project is in trouble before it even begins. If your customers don't have time to tell you why you are writing this software for them in the first place, maybe it shouldn't be written at all.*

STUDENT: *Are you saying we should stop the project?*

MASTER: *I am saying that to have a successful project, you need customer and stakeholder commitment. And that without it, you are already stalled whether you like it or not.*

STUDENT: *If this is the case, then what should I do?*

MASTER: *You need to clearly, and forcefully, explain to your customers what it is going to take to make this project a success. Their involvement, commitment, and engagement are required. This may not be the time for this project. Perhaps they really are busy and simply have too much on their plate. If this is the case, tell them that you will be here for them when they are ready. Until then, you have other customers to serve.*

STUDENT: *Thank you, Sensei. I will think about this more.*

What's Next?

Before we go any further, let's stop to take a breather.

Can you feel it?
Can you see what is happening here?

With each passing inception deck exercise, the spirit and scope of the project are becoming more clear.

- We now know the *why* behind our project.
- We have a good elevator pitch.
- We know what our product box would look like.
- We're putting some stakes in the ground around scope.
- We have a pretty good idea about who's in our neighborhood.

Now I know what you're thinking. Enough context already! When will we get down to business and start talking about how we are going to build this thing? And the answer is right now.

In Chapter 5, *Making It Real*, on page 57, we are going to start to visualize what the technical solution for your project is going to look like and what it's going to take to deliver.

So, turn the page, and get ready to start making it real.

Making It Real

Now that we've got the *why*, we can start getting smart about the *how*. In these sections of the inception deck, we are going to start getting more concrete with our solution and start putting some stakes in the ground.

Here, we are going to do the following:

- Present a technical solution
- Look at some risks
- Size things up
- Be clear on what has to give (something always has to give)
- Show our sponsors what this project is really going to take

But let's start first by getting real with the solution.

5.1 Show Your Solution

Visualizing the solution is about getting a read on what we're going up against technically and making sure everyone is cool with how we are going to build this thing.

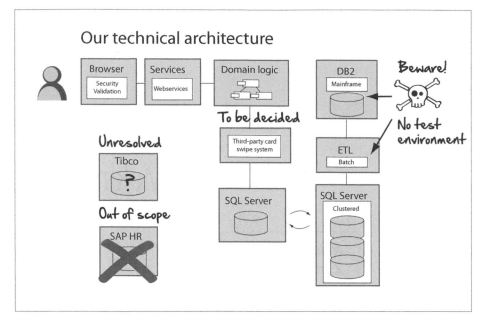

Talking about your solution and getting it out there in front of your team and customer is good for a number of reasons:

- It sets expectations around tools and technology.
- It visualizes assumptions around project boundaries and scope.
- It communicates risk.

Even if you suspect everyone is on board with your solution, put it up there for all to see anyway. Worst case, you will reconfirm what everyone knows. Best case, you save yourself a lot of pain by not betting the farm on something that turns out not to be true.

How Does It Work?

You just get together with the technical folks on your team and talk about how you are going to build this thing. You draw architectural diagrams, play what-if scenarios, and generally try to get a feel for how big and how complex this thing is.

If there are open source or proprietary frameworks you are thinking about using, share those with the team (some companies limit which open source tools they allow).

But that's basically it. Draw enough pictures to show everyone how you are going to build the system, set expectations around the risky areas, and make sure everyone is on board with the technical solution.

> ## You Pick Your Architecture When You Pick Your Team
>
> To a team with a big hammer, everything looks like a nail.
>
> A team strong in databases will naturally want to do most of the heavy lifting in SQL, while a team strong in object-oriented design (OO) will want to put all the complexity in there.
>
> So if you've picked your team, you've already taken a big step toward picking your architecture whether you like it or not.
>
> That's why it's important that you telegraph your technical punches early—not because your solution is perfect or you have all the answers but more because you want to get the right people on your project and ensure they are aligned with your proposed solution.

5.2   Ask What Keeps Us Up at Night

Project risks

- Director of construction availability
- Team not co-located
- New security architecture
- Timing of new logistics tracking system

Many a manager has lost a good night's sleep over the state of a software project—and with good reason. Estimates can be overly optimistic. Customers can (and do) continuously change their minds. There always seem to be more things to do than time and money allow. And these are the project risks we know about!

Asking ourselves *what keeps us up and night* invites a healthy discussion about some of the challenges you and the team might face when you're delivering and what you can do to prevent them from ever seeing the light of day.

Why Talking About Risk Is Good

Talking about project risk is one of those things that most people would rather skip when starting projects. No one wants to look like Chicken Little, running around saying the sky is falling.

But talking about risk is a great way of letting people know what you need for the success of your project.

Take co-location, for example. To someone in facilities, who has never worked on a software project before, not having everyone sitting together may not be such a big deal.

To an agile project, however, co-location is king, and talking about risks is your chance to throw your cards on the table and make it very clear that if the following are true, then all bets are off on the success of this project:

- You don't have a co-located team.
- You don't have an engaged customer.
- You don't have control over your own development environment.
- You don't have something else that you think you need to be successful.

This is your chance to take a stand and ask for what you need. You may not get everything you'd like, but at least you've made the case and set expectations with everyone about the consequences of not doing what you suggest.

Here are some other good reasons for talking about risk early in the project:

> ## Bloomberg on Risk
>
> Michael Bloomberg should know a thing or two about risk. As the founder of the Bloomberg financial company and the mayor of New York, he has had to navigate some pretty shark-infested waters.
>
> In *Bloomberg by Bloomberg [Blo01]*, Michael explains his favorite technique for handling risk:
>
> 1. Write everything down that could possibly go wrong.
> 2. Think really hard about how to stop those things from happening.
> 3. Then tear it up.
>
> Michael's philosophy is that you can never see everything coming and that no plan is perfect. Life is going to throw curveballs and sliders at you that you don't get to bat against in the practice cage. Get used to it. Either you know what's coming or you don't and never will. For the rest, just take it as it comes.

- It highlights project challenges early.

  The time to talk about risk is now—at the beginning. It's too late once the bomb has gone off. If you have any issues or have seen any showstoppers, now is the time to air them.

- It gives you a chance to call the craziness.

  If you heard some crazy talk over the course of doing the inception deck, this is your chance to call it out.

- It just feels good.

  There is something good about sharing and discussing your fears with others. It gives the team a chance to bond, share war stories, and just learn from each others' experiences.

Remember, you have a lot of leeway here at the beginning of the project, and this is your chance to lay it on the line. Use it.

Identify Those Risks Worth Sweating

Get together with your team (including your customer) and brainstorm all the possible risks you could see happening on your project. You are the sword your customer is going to be swinging on this project, so anything that's going to affect your ability to chop would be good for them to hear.

Then with your great big list, take all your risks and split them into two categories: those worth sweating and those that aren't.

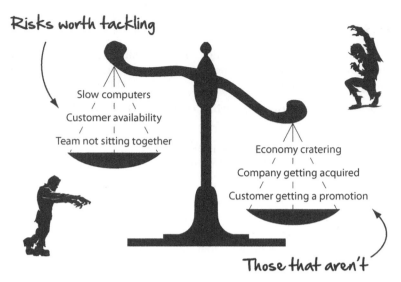

For example, although there is a slim chance the entire economy could crash and we could all be out of jobs, it's not something we can really do anything about. So, don't sweat it.

Losing our lead programmer in a hot job market, however, could happen. So, we will want to take steps to ensure that knowledge is being shared and no one becomes too specialized in one area.

And for those moments when you're feeling overwhelmed or struggling to figure out whether a particular issue is worth the sweat, there's always the serenity prayer:

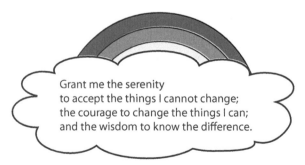

Grant me the serenity
to accept the things I cannot change;
the courage to change the things I can;
and the wisdom to know the difference.

5.3 Size It Up

This is about trying to figure out whether we have a one-, three-, or six-month project on our hands. We can't get much more precise than that at this point in our project, but we still need to give our sponsors some idea of when they can expect their software to be delivered, even if it is only a really rough guess.

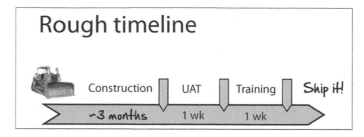

We'll go over all the details of how agile estimation works in Chapter 7, *Estimation: The Fine Art of Guessing*, on page 99. But for now, pretend the team has already done the estimates for the project, and here we are just presenting the results.

Before we do that, though, let's first go over the importance of thinking small.

Think Small

You may not have heard of him, but Randy Mott is kind of a rock star in the Fortune 500 world. Randy helped develop the world-famous Wal-Mart data warehouse/inventory system that lets store managers track in real time what flavor of Pop-Tart is selling best at any given store in the country. He did the same thing at Dell, allowing Dell to quickly spot rising inventory and offer discounts on overstocked items. And now as CIO of HP, Randy is helping facilitate HP's $1 billion makeover of its internal systems.

Randy obviously did a lot of things right to help companies like Wal-Mart, Dell, and HP get to where they are. But one of his self-proclaimed secrets was the insistence that no development cycle take longer than six months:

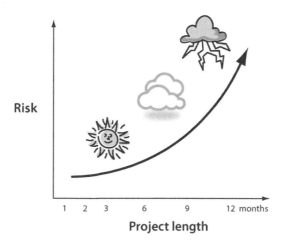

The problem with large, open-ended projects is they seem to perpetually over-promise and under-deliver. There is always one more thing to add or one more feature to be included. And before long costs escalate, estimates are thrown out the window, and the project collapses under the girth of its own ever-expanding weight.

Randy's sweet spot for IT projects is six months or less. Anything longer he finds too risky. That doesn't mean every IT initiative he wanted to deliver could be built in six months. He just realized he had been burned enough times to know that if he wanted to deliver something really big, he needed to break it down into smaller, more manageable pieces.

Randy and agile sing from the same song sheet when it comes to sizing up IT projects: the smaller, the better—preferably six months or less.

Set Some Expectations About Size

Sizing it up basically involves looking at your estimates and coming up with a rough plan for your stakeholders. You have to factor in user acceptance testing (UAT), training, and anything else you need to do before going live. But all you are really doing is giving them a best guess of how big you think this thing is and whether it can be done in a reasonable period of time.

You have a couple of options when it comes to presenting your plan. You can put a stake in the ground and say you are going to deliver by date. Or you can commit to delivering a core set of features and be more flexible on the date. We'll cover the differences between the two and when you would want to choose one or the other in *Step 5: Pick Some Dates*, on page 126.

Note: Under no conditions can you let your customer think the plans you are presenting here are hard commitments. They are not. They are simply unvalidated high-level guesses that can be vetted only by building something, measuring how long that takes, and feeding that information back into the plan.

5.4   Be Clear on What's Going to Give

There are certain laws and forces that demand respect on our projects. Budgets and dates tend to be fixed. Scope regularly seems to increase with reckless abandon. And quality is always #1.

Yet these forces are often in conflict. Giving in to one means taking something away from the others. If left unbalanced for too long, the force of one can overwhelm a project until it finally breaks and snaps.

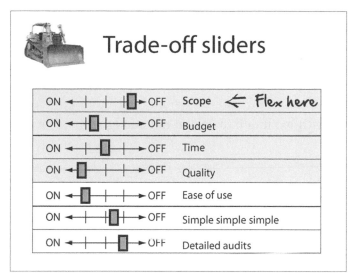

Something has to give. The question is what?

Agile has a way of taming these wild and dangerous forces, and I am going to leave you in the capable hands of Master Sensei to show you how.

Together, you will study which forces are in play on our projects, the trade-offs they force us to make, and how you can use their power for the good of your project.

The Test

1. Which of these forces is most precious to a software project?

- a) Quality.
- b) Time.
- c) Scope.
- d) Budget.

2. When faced with too much to do and not enough time, is it better to do the following:

- a) Cut scope
- b) Add more people to the project
- c) Push out the release date
- d) Sacrifice quality

3. Which is most painful?

- a) Walking on fire
- b) Chewing broken glass
- c) Doing the Macarena
- d) Asking your sponsor for more money

How did you feel answering these questions?

Did you find yourself thinking, "It depends"?

There are no absolute right or wrong answers to these questions. They are intended to show you that there are forces at work on your project and striking the right balance between them takes work.

It is time you learned about these forces and how to tame them. It is time you learned the secrets of...the Furious Four.

The Furious Four

Since the dawn of time, all projects have been bound and governed by four interwoven and connected forces. They are known as the Furious Four: time, budget, quality, and scope.

With us on every project, they are there causing mayhem and mischief every time:

- Our schedules get squeezed.
- Our budgets get cut.
- Our bug list grows.
- We have too much to do.

As fierce as the Furious Four are, however, they can be tamed. Let's now consider each in turn and how we might work with them harmoniously on our projects.

Time

Time is finite. We can neither create it nor store it. We must simply do our best with that which is given.

That is why agile warriors favor time-boxing their delivery efforts. A warrior knows that continuously pushing out release dates and delaying the shipment of valuable software reduces the customer's return on investment and runs the risk of never releasing anything at all—the worst possible fate for any software project.

And so the agile warrior fixes time.

Budget

Budget is the twin of time. It too is fixed, finite, and usually not forthcoming in abundance.

One of the most difficult things for a customer to do is to go to the sponsor and ask for more money. It does happen on occasion—but the experience is never pleasant.

To avoid this unpleasantness, the warrior treats budget the same way as time. Fixed.

Quality

There are those who believe quality can be sacrificed in the interest of time. They are wrong. Any short-term gain in speed, resulting from a reduction in quality, is a false and temporary illusion.

Reducing quality is like juggling flaming machetes on a cold winter's day. Yes, we may warm our hands briefly for a few moments, but at some point we are going to cut ourselves and get badly burned.

And so quality too is fixed and always held to the highest standard.

Training vs. Delivery

Training vs. delivery was something we always had to balance on projects at ThoughtWorks. Although we never viewed ourselves as a training company, it was a good hook for our sales guys, and it got us in the door to a lot of places.

However, training is one thing. Delivery is another.

By using the slider board and asking the customer to rank these two competing forces, we could set expectations with the customer and act accordingly.

Scope

With time, budget, and quality fixed, the agile warrior is left but with one force around which to bend on a project: scope.

If there is too much to do, the warrior will do less. If reality disagrees with the plan, the warrior will change the plan instead of reality.

This makes some of my students uncomfortable. Many come to my dojo having been taught that plans are fixed, immovable, rigid things, never to be changed or altered. Nothing could be further from the truth.

A date may be fixed. But a plan is not.

And so, out of the four forces arrayed against him, the agile warrior will fix time, budget, and quality, and flex the project around scope.

You are now ready for the trade-off sliders.

The Trade-off Sliders

The ancient trade-off sliders are one tool a warrior can use to enter discussion with their customer about the impact of the Furious Four on their project.

For example, the warrior will want to gain insight into how their customer views things like time, budget, and quality. Likewise, the warrior will want to set expectations around the importance of being flexible on scope and not get too married to all the features (user stories) on the to-do (master story) list.

Make sure they understand you are going to be flexible on scope

Once the forces are named and plain for all to see, the warrior will ask their customers to rank these forces in order of relative importance. No two forces can occupy the same level of ranking (in other words, they can't all be #1).

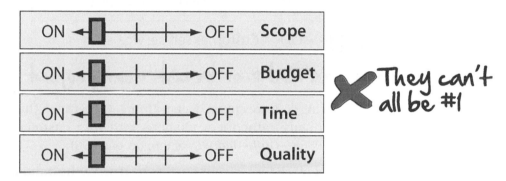

They can't all be #1

Most customers understand that something has to give on their projects. Should they become nervous about ranking them, remind them that everything on the board is important. In other words, just because quality has a lower ranking than time doesn't mean quality is not important. We are simply communicating that we can't miss our ship date—no matter what. Hence, time has the higher ranking.

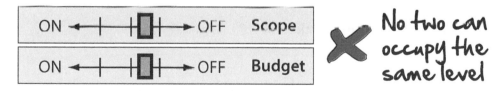

No two can occupy the same level

As important as the Furious Four are, however, there are other forces we must also keep at bay. Let's now see what other forces might be at work on your projects.

On Time and on Budget Are Not Enough

Consider this:

- What good is the computer game that is no fun to play?
- Does an online dating community exist if there is no one there to court?
- What sound does an online radio station make if no one is listening?

As important as it is to maintain balance among the Furious Four, the whole story they do not tell. There are other forces at work on our projects of equal if not greater value.

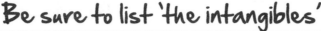

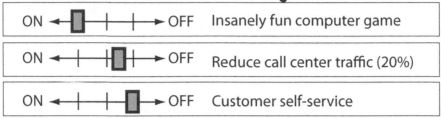

You may have felt them during your inception deck training. Or perhaps they were hinted at during your story-gathering workshops with your customer (Section 6.4, *How to Host a Story-Gathering Workshop*, on page 93).

When you present the trade-off sliders to your customer, reserve the bottom level for those "intangibles" that will make or break your project.

Only by making them visible and putting them up for all to see will you demonstrate you truly understand that which is most important to your customer.

Phew! You made it. Let's see how we can bring it all together now in one final plan and present to our sponsors what it's going to take.

5.5 Show What It's Going to Take

You are almost there!

You've got the vision.

You've got the plan.

Now you just have to figure out what it's going to take and how much it's going to cost.

In this section, you are going to lay it all out before your sponsors. This is the team. This is the plan. And this is how much it is going to cost.

Let's start with the team.

Assemble Your A-Team

At this point in the game you'll have a pretty good idea what kind of team you are going to need to pull this mission off. Here we simply want to spell it out.

#	Role	Competencies/Expectations
1	UX designer	Capable of rapid prototyping (paper prototypes) Wireframes & mockups, user flows, HTML/CSS a plus
1	Project manager	Comfortable with ambiguity Can function without going command and control
3	Developers	C#, ASP.NET, MVC experience Unit testing, TDD, refactoring, continuous integration
1	Analyst	Comfortable with just-in-time analysis XP-style story card development Willing to help test
1	Customer	Available one hour a day for questions Can meet once per week for feedback Able to direct, steer, and make decisions about project
1	Tester	Automated testing experience Works well with developers & customer Good at exploratory testing

This is a good time to talk about roles and responsibilities (Chapter 2, *Meet Your Agile Team*, on page 13) and what is going to be expected of everyone when they join this project.

One role I usually spend a few extra minutes on is the customer. First, it's super-important, and second, it's not really baked into most companies' DNA.

Here I like to look the customer in the eye and make sure they understand what they're signing up for when they choose to join an agile project.

Can they commit the time?
Are they empowered to make the necessary decisions?
Are they willing to direct and steer the development of this project?

Developers, testers, and analysts can usually figure out their new roles. But the agile customer is new for some, so it's worth emphasizing.

One other thing you'll want to be clear on (especially if you have multiple stakeholders) is who's calling the shots.

Clarify Who's Calling the Shots

There's nothing more confusing to a team than not knowing who to take their marching orders from.

The director of IT wants to prove the latest technology. The VP of strategy wants to be first to market. The VP of sales just publicly committed to a new version for the second quarter.

You can't have multiple stakeholders, all approaching the team with different ideas about where the team should be headed, what the priorities are, and what to work on next.

Instead, you want to make it very clear up front who's driving the bus. That doesn't mean other stakeholders don't have a say—far from it. We just want the customer to speak to the team in one voice.

By putting this slide up and raising this issue now, you can avoid a lot of confusion and costly rework and realignment later.

Even if you think you know who is calling the shots, ask anyway. Not only will this remove any doubt, it will also make it crystal clear to the team and the other stakeholders who the ultimate decider really is.

Now let's talk about money.

Estimate How Much It's Going to Cost

You may never need to talk about money on your project. Your budget may have already been set, and you will simply be told how much you have to work with.

If you do need to create a rough budget for your project, however, here's a quick and easy way to get some rough numbers:

Simply multiply the number of team members over the duration of your project, at some blended rate, and *voila*—you have your budget.

Sure, you may have some software costs, and yes, your company may have a special way of accounting for this or that. But almost without a doubt, the greatest cost to your project walks on two legs and sits at a computer.

Now let's bring it all together and help them make that go/no-go decision.

Bringing It All Together

This is the slide most stakeholders will be super-keen on because at the end of the day there's only two questions they really need answered:

- When is it going to be done?
- How much is it going to cost?

To be clear, we can't commit 100 percent to these dates and numbers at the moment. Yes, we've done some great homework, and sure, we've answered some fundamental questions, but there are simply too many unknowns at this point (like how fast the team can go) to treat these numbers as anything other than best guesses.

One way to present the numbers is in a slide like that presented at the beginning of the section. If it's a program of projects, or something bigger, use your creativity and ask yourself what you'd like to see if it were your money, you were the head honcho, and you needed to decide whether this project was a go.

Inception Deck Wrap-Up

Congratulations! You made it! You've just completed your first crucial step to successfully defining, getting people aligned, and kick-starting your very own agile project.

Just look at the picture and story you, your team, your sponsor, and your customer can now share and tell. Collectively, you all know the following:

- What you are building and why
- What's compelling about your project
- What big rocks you need to move
- Who's in your neighborhood
- What your solution looks like
- What major challenges and risks you're going to face
- How big this thing is
- Where you are prepared to bend and flex
- Approximately what it is going to take (time and money)

Master Sensei
and the
aspiring warrior

MASTER: *Tell me what you have learned so far regarding the inception deck.*

STUDENT: *I now see the importance of asking the tough questions at the start of a project and seeking alignment before the project begins.*

MASTER: *Very good. What else?*

STUDENT: *I now see that project chartering doesn't have to take months of scoping and planning. With the inception deck, we can scope and set expectations quickly, usually within a couple of days.*

MASTER: *And what if something important in spirit, scope, or intent of a project changes? What should we do then?*

STUDENT: *Update the deck. Run it by everyone again, and ensure the alignment and shared understanding is still there.*

MASTER: *Very good. You are ready for the next stage of your journey.*

What's Next?

With the *why* of your project, we are now going to go over a few of the details we glossed over earlier in the chapter.

In agile planning, we are going to go over everything you'll need to create your very own agile project plan. Estimation, master story lists, concepts like team velocity—we're going to cover it all.

And there is no better place to start than with the unit of work from which all agile projects are made—the humble user story.

Part III

Agile Project Planning

CHAPTER 6

Gathering User Stories

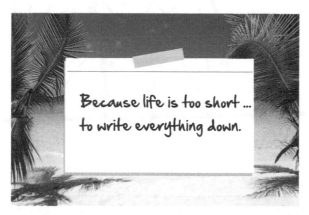

Because life is too short ...
to write everything down.

In Part III we are going to get into the basics of agile planning: user stories, estimation, and adaptive planning.

By learning how to gather requirements as user stories, you will see how agile plans are always kept up-to-date, contain only the latest and greatest information, and avoid one of the greatest wastes our industry has ever known—premature up-front analysis.

Let's start by looking at how we used to gather requirements and some of the challenges that come with trying to write everything down.

6.1   The Problem with Documentation

Heavy documentation as a means of capturing requirements has never really worked for software projects. Customers seldom get what they want. Teams seldom build what is needed. And vast amounts of time and energy are spent debating what was written, instead of doing what needs to be done.

Here are some other problems teams run into when they rely too heavily on documentation for their software requirements:

What If We Just Tried Documenting More?

The problem with gathering requirements as documentation isn't one of volume —it's one of communication. First, you can't have a conversation with a document (at least not a very engaging one).

Second, it's just really easy to misinterpret what someone wrote.

I didn't say she took the money.	
I, didn't say she took the money.	I didn't say it.
I didn't **say** she took the money.	I said something else ...
I didn't say **she** took the money.	But someone else might have!
I didn't say she **took** the money.	She spent it instead.
I didn't say she took **the money**.	Nope. Instead she stole my heart and left for San Francisco.
Words are slippery things!	

> ## Is a Requirement Really a Requirement?
>
> Agile warriors don't believe in requirements. The term is just plain wrong, as Kent Beck, one of the great agile warriors puts it in *Extreme Programming Explained: Embrace Change [Bec00]*:
>
> "Software development has been steered wrong by the term requirement, defined in the dictionary as something that is mandatory or obligatory. The word carries a connotation of absolutism and permanence, inhibitors for embracing change. And the word "requirement" is just plain wrong.
>
> "Out of the thousands of pages used to describe requirements, if you deliver the right 5, 10 or 20 percent, you will likely realize all of the business benefit envisioned for the whole system. So what were the other 80 percent? Not requirements—they weren't mandatory or obligatory."

I remember Martin Fowler once lamenting that even after spending years working on a book, he was continually surprised by the number of times people missed the core message of what he was trying to say.

In extreme cases, mistakes in grammar cost companies millions of dollars.[1] But mostly, they just serve as a poor means of describing and capturing what customers would like to see in their software.

This leads us to one of the most important principles of agile:

Agile principle

The most efficient and effective method of conveying information to and within a development team is face-to-face conversation.

So, what we need is something that enables us to have a conversation about a requirement, captures the essence of what our customer wants, and is small enough for planning yet descriptive enough to remind us what we are talking about.

6.2 Enter the User Story

Agile *user stories* are short descriptions of features our customer would like to one day see in their software. They are usually written on small index cards

---

1. http://www.nytimes.com/2006/10/25/business/worldbusiness/25comma.html

(to remind us not to try to write everything down) and are there to encourage us to get off our butts and go talk to our customers.

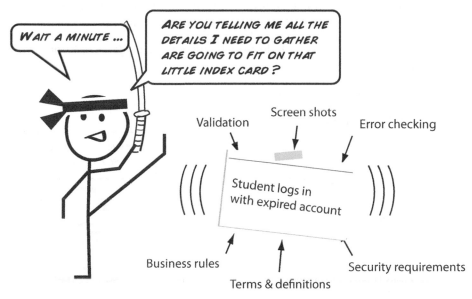

When you first see an agile user story, you may be tempted to ask, "Where's the beef?" Don't be fooled. The beef is there—just not where you think it is.

Not exactly—more that they don't have to.

Agile encourages teams to use index cards (small recipe cards) to remind teams that the initial goal of the requirements-gathering exercise isn't to get into all the details. It's to write down a few key words to capture the spirit of the feature and file it away for a later date.

Why capture just a few key words and not go to town on the full requirement? It's because we don't know at this point when we are going to get to that feature or whether we are even going to need it! We may not get to this feature for months. And by the time we do, the world, and our software, is going to look a lot different.

So, to save us the time and energy of going pro on it now and having to redo it all later, we defer diving into the low-level details until later (more on this in Section 9.4, *Step 1: Analysis and Design: Making the Work Ready*, on page 147).

So, think of a user story as a promise of a conversation. At some point, we'll do the deep dive and get in there. But we're not going to do it until we are sure we're going to need it.

6.3 Elements of Good User Stories

The first element of a good user story is that it's something of value to our customers. What's valuable? Something they would pay for.

For example, which restaurant do you think your hungry customer would rather dine at?

Ernie's Tech Diner

C++	3 days

The system will be written in C++.

Connection pooling	2 days

All database access will be handled by a database connection pool.

Model-View-Presenter pattern	5 days

The system will separate presentation logic from business logic.

Sam's Business Pancake House

Create user account	3 days

Users will have individual, personalized accounts to log into your system.

Notify subscribers of new listings	2 days

Subscribers will be notified every time a new house is listed in their market.

Cancel subscription	1 day

Embedded in every email will be an unsubscribed option.

User stories have to make sense to business. That's why we always try to write them in simple terms that they understand and stay away from any technical mumbo jumbo.

That doesn't mean that we can't use connection pooling or design patterns when building our systems. It means that it's better if we put it in terms that they understand.

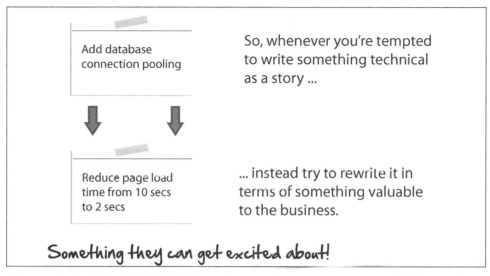

The second characteristic of a really good user story is one that goes from end to end—or as we like to call it, "slices the cake."

UMMM CAKE ... OM NOM NOM

Just like most of us wouldn't want the cake without the icing, our customers don't want a half or a third of a solution. That's why a good user story goes end-to-end slicing through all the layers of the architecture and delivers something of value.

Good user stories also have the following characteristics:

Independent

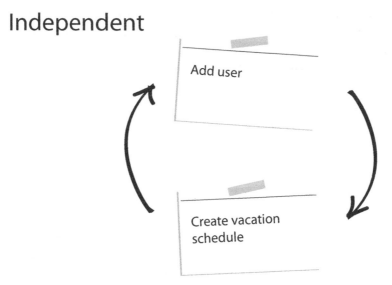

Things change on projects. What was really important last week can suddenly becomes not so important this week. If all of our stories are intertwined and dependent on one another, making trade-offs becomes hard.

We don't always succeed (we need an application before we can create the reports), but slicing our stories from end to end and gathering them by feature enables us to treat the vast majority of our stories as independent and be flexible on scope when necessary.

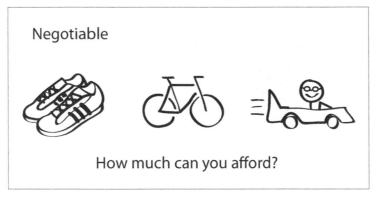

There are always multiple ways to deliver any given story. We could build the Ford Focus, Honda Accord, or Porsche 911 version of any given feature.

Negotiable stories are nice because they give us the wiggle room we sometimes need to work within our budgets. Sometimes we will need the Porsche. Other times the more spartan Ford will do.

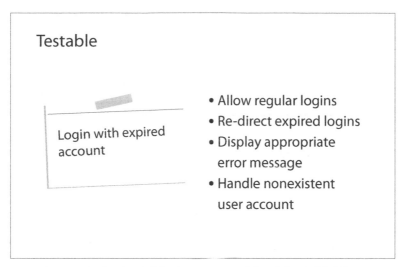

We like our stories to be testable (as opposed to detestable) because we like to know when something is working. By writing tests against our user stories, we give the development team a stake in the ground and a way of knowing when they are done.

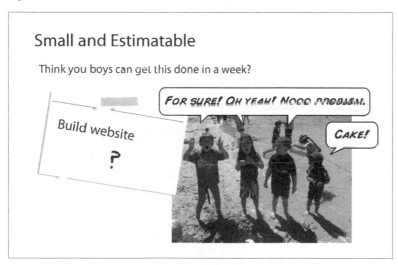

And speaking of done, how do we know a story will fit in within the time frames we have? By making our stories small (one to five days), we can ensure they can fit into our one- to two-week iterations, which will enable us to estimate more confidently.

Thanks to Bill Wake for coming up with the handy INVEST acronym for "Independent, Negotiable, Valuable, Estimatable, Small, and Testable."

In summary, here are what user stories give us when compared to documentation for gathering requirements:

User stories	Specifications & requirement docs
Lean, accurate, just-in-time	Heavy, inaccurate, out-of-date
Encourage face-to-face communication	Encourage guesswork (false assumptions)
Simplified planning	Complex planning
Cheap, fast, easy to create	Expensive, slow, hard to create
Never out-of-date	Always out-of-date
Based on latest learnings	Based on little or no learning
Enable real-time feedback	Disable real-time feedback
Avoid false sense of accuracy	Promote false sense of accuracy
Allow for team-based collaboration and innovation	Discourage open collaboration and innovation

That's enough theory. Let's get real and gather some stories for a local dude getting ready for the summer surf scene.

Welcome to Big Wave Dave's Surf Shop

Dave hired a local company a few months ago to build a website, but they spent the budget writing up the requirements (surprise!) and never got around to actually building the website (sheesh!). Fortunately, Dave has come to us for help.

It's OK to Help Customers Write Stories

Don't take earlier agile books too literally when they tell you that customers should write all the user stories. That advice is right in spirit—but not in practice.

It's true that customers should provide the content for our user stories (because they are the ones who know what they want built). In practice, however, it will be you who will be doing most of the writing.

So, don't be worried if you find yourself giving them a hand. Just make sure your customers are active participants in the process and you are capturing their needs in the cards.

Let's Find Out What Dave Needs

Sitting down with Dave, we ask him to list all the features he would like to see on his website. This is nothing too deep—just high-level descriptions of features he would like his website to have and things he would like it to do.

First, I want the website to be a place for the local scene. Somewhere the kids can come and check out upcoming events—surf competitions, lessons, things like that.

Second, I need a place to sell merchandise. Boards, wet suits, clothes, videos, and things like that. But it's gotta be easy to use and look really good.

Third, I've always wanted a webcam pointing at the beach. This way, you don't have to come down to check out the conditions. You can just open your laptop, go to the website, and see whether it's worth getting up. This also means the website has to be fast.

See whether you can extract six user stories based on Dave's description of his website (Figure 3, *Extracting User Stories*, on page 90. Don't worry about writing perfect stories. Just practice taking what your customer says they would like to see in their software and extracting user stories from what you hear.

Now looking at each one of your stories, how did they measure up against our INVEST criteria (Independent, Negotiable, Valuable, Estimatable, Small, and Testable)?

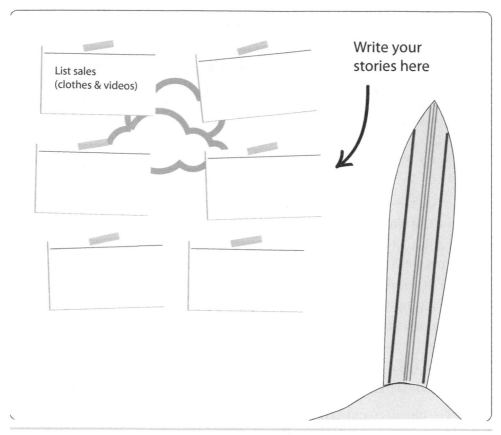

List sales
(clothes & videos)

Write your
stories here

Figure 3—Extracting User Stories

Don't worry if they aren't perfect (they never are). Just get used to grabbing the idea, making sure it's something your customer understands and would find value in, and writing it down on a card.

Let's pretend our first pass through the story list looked something like Figure 4, *User Stories Extracted*, on page 91.

What do you think about the last two stories on our list?

- The website must be super-fast!
- The design should look really good.

Are these good stories? Why not?

If you are thinking *The website must be super-fast!* is a little vague and ambiguous, you're right! How fast is super-fast? How do we test for whether something *looks really good*?

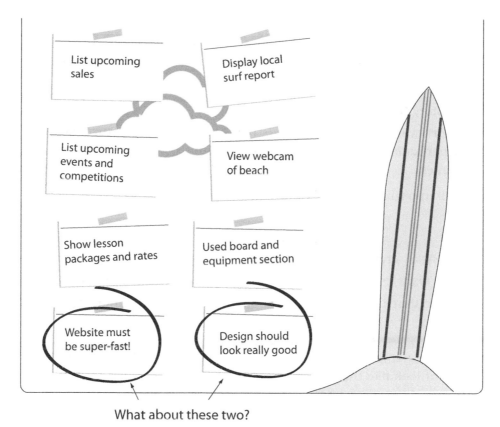

What about these two?

Figure 4—User Stories Extracted

Stories like these, we call *constraints*. They aren't your typical user stories that we can deliver in a week. But they are important because they describe characteristics our customers would like to see in their software.

Sometimes, we'll be able to translate these into testable stories. For example, we could rewrite *The website must be super-fast!* like this:

That is certainly clearer (because we now know what super-fast means). And we can certainly write tests for that.

Constraints are important, but they don't form the bulk of our user stories. Capture them on different colored cards. Make sure everyone on the team is aware of them, and test for them periodically while you're developing your software.

The User Story Template

A few short, well-chosen words are usually enough to remind the team about what a particular user story was about. Some teams, however, like a little more context.

If you fall into this camp, try using this user story template:

As a <type of user>   **who**   is this story for
I want <some goal>   ➡   **what** they want to do
so that <some reason>.   **why**   they want to do it

For example, using the template, some of our stories for Big Wave Dave's surf shop might look like this:

As a surfer who likes to sleep,
I want to check local surf conditions via a webcam
so that I don't have to get out of bed if there is no swell.

As a land-locked Canadian hockey player,
I want to sign up for some adrenaline-pumping lessons
so I can feel the thrill of going "over the falls."

As a grommet looking for the latest surf wear,
I want to see all the latest board shorts and designs
so that I can look stylin' for the Sheilas this summer.

The nice thing about the user story template is it answers three important questions about the user story: the who, the what, and the why. It gives a little more context and really emphasizes and focuses on the business, which is a good thing.

The disadvantage of the story is all the extra verbiage makes it harder to parse and figure out what the story is about. Some people like the extra context. Others find it too much noise.

Try them both and see what you like—it doesn't have to be one or the other. For example, you could use a short name like "Add user" for planning and then on the back of the card the longer template version for analysis later if that helps.

6.4 How to Host a Story-Gathering Workshop

Now, before we can go off and create our agile project plan, we need a list of all the features our customers think they would like to see in their software. One way to do this is to host a *story-gathering workshop*—a venue for the development team and customer to get together and write user stories about the system they would like to build.

The goal of the story-gathering workshop is breadth. You want to cast your net wide and discover as many features as possible. It is not because you are necessarily going to build them all; it's more because you want to get everything on the table and make sure you have the big picture.

The NOT list (Section 4.4, *Create a NOT List*, on page 50) you created as part of the inception deck can help you get going here. But it usually comes down to sitting down with your customer, drawing some pictures, and writing story cards as you talk about the system. That's it!

Here are some tips on how to host a good story-gathering workshop.

Step 1: Get a Big Open Room

You want something you can get up and move around in—a room where you can stick pictures on the wall, collect cards on a big open table, and do whatever it takes to get the story discovery juices flowing.

Step 2: Draw Lots of Pictures

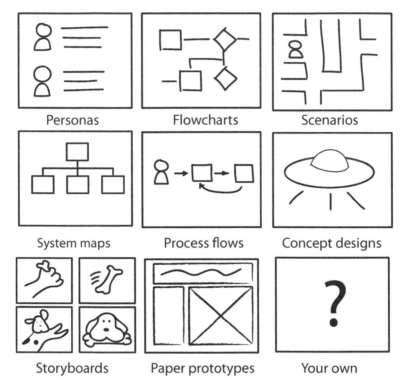

Pictures are a great way to brainstorm ideas about the system and are a treasure trove for discovering stories.

Personas (descriptions of the people who are going to be using your system) are good for getting to know your customers. Flowcharts, process flows, and scenarios are great for role playing and really getting a feel for how the system needs to work. System maps and information architecture diagrams help organize and break down the work. And concept designs and paper prototypes are cheap ways of just trying stuff out and seeing what works.

Remember, we're shooting for breadth here. So, be careful not to dive too deep on the details—you want to keep it high level.

But once you have a few good pictures and an understanding of how the system needs to work, you're ready to start mining the pictures for stories.

Step 3: Write Lots of Stories

Using your new diagrams and pictures, walk through them with your customer, extracting user stories as you go.

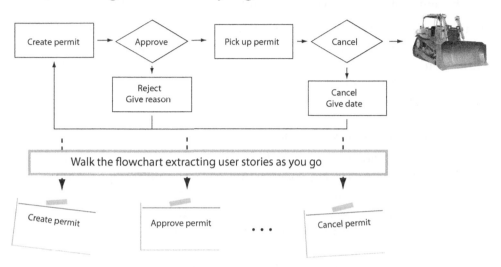

If most of your application hangs off one or two screens, take those screens and break them down into smaller pieces of functionality.

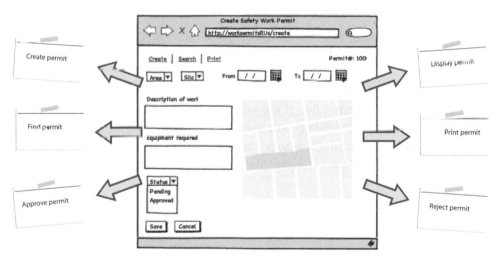

From one flow chart, backed by a few lo-fi paper prototypes, you can usually get the most of the core stories for your project.

When you're extracting your user stories, look for small, discrete, end-to-end pieces of functionality (usually one to five days worth of effort). It's OK if some of your stories are kind of big. We call these *epics*—big stories that take a couple weeks of work.

Epics are handy for high-level planning or for capturing big stories that we think we may have to take on but are not really sure yet. If you have some major pieces of functionality like this, treat them like any other story, and break them down if and when they come up for development.

At the end of the day, ten to forty high-level stories are usually enough for three to six months of planning. If your stories number in the hundreds, either you're planning too far ahead or you're going into too much detail. We are shooting for breadth (not depth) here. So, don't dive too deep and get lost in the weeds.

Step 4: Brainstorm Everything Else

As good as the pictures are, they don't capture everything we need to do on your project: data migration, load testing, SOX compliance paper work, production support documentation, training materials, two weeks for user acceptance testing (UAT), and so on. All these things and more need to be captured in the cards and prioritized and treated like any other deliverable for project.

This is a good time to pull out your picture from Section 4.5, *Meet Your Neighbors*, on page 52 and brainstorm all the other things you are going to need to do to make this project a huge success.

If there is something you need to do (even if it's not software related), create a card for it and write it down.

Step 5: Scrub the List and Make It Shine

Once you have your initial list, it's good to go through it a few times looking for duplicates, looking for things you may have missed, grouping logical stories together, and consolidating it into a simple, easy-to-understand to-do list of things you need to deliver. Congratulations! You now have the beginning of your project plan!

Master Sensei and the aspiring warrior

STUDENT: *Master, if face-to-face communication is the most efficient way of sharing information about the system, does that mean I should spend more time talking to my customer about their requirements and less time writing them down?*

MASTER: *That is correct.*

STUDENT: *Does this mean I should never use documentation when gathering requirements?*

MASTER: *No. The goal isn't the elimination of all documentation—documentation is neither good nor bad. The goal is to remind ourselves of that which is most effective for sharing information about our project.*

STUDENT: *So, some documentation is permitted when gathering requirements?*

MASTER: *Of course. Just do not make it your primary focus. Instead, concentrate on understanding your customer and what they need from their software. Know the limits of documentation as you describe. Make it your last resort for understanding. Not your first.*

STUDENT: *Thank you, Master. I will meditate on this more.*

What's Next?

Well done, amigo! Now that you see user stories are nothing more than short descriptions of features our customers would like to see in their software, you are one step away from being able to create your very first agile project plan.

In the next chapter on estimation, we'll see how to size our stories so they can withstand the inevitable hiccups we encounter during delivery.

So, onward and upward, as we demystify the art and science behind agile estimation.

CHAPTER 7

Estimation: The Fine Art of Guessing

Get ready to bring some reality back to the estimation process. Agile dispenses with the pleasantries and reminds us what our initial high-level estimates really are—really, they're bad guesses.

But by learning how to estimate the agile way, you'll stop trying to get something your up-front estimates can't give (precision and accuracy) and instead focus on what really matters—building a plan you and your customer can work with and believe in.

In this chapter, you'll learn how to estimate your user stories the agile way, as well as some powerful group estimation techniques for sizing up things.

7.1 The Problem with High-Level Estimates

Let's face it. Our industry has had some challenges when it comes to setting expectations around estimates on software projects.

It's not that our estimates are necessarily wrong (though they almost always are). It's more that people have looked to estimates for something they can never give—an accurate prediction of the future.

> ## The Point of Estimation
>
> "The primary purpose of software estimation is not to predict a project's outcome; it is to determine whether a project's targets are realistic enough to allow the project to be controlled to meet them."
>
> —Steve McConnell, *Software Estimation: Demystifying the Black Art* [McC06]

JOHNSON! GET ME A DETAILED ESTIMATE FOR OUR ...

YET TO BE SPEC'D SYSTEM, USING OUR
YET TO BE DETERMINED TECHNOLOGY, WITH OUR
YET TO BE DETERMINED TEAM, IN OUR
YET TO BE DETERMINED BUSINESS ENVIRONMENT
TO BE BUILT NEXT YEAR.

It's like somewhere along the way, people lost sight of the fact that

HIGH-LEVEL ESTIMATES ARE GUESSES
(AND USUALLY REALLY BAD, OVERLY OPTIMISTIC ONES AT THAT)

And it is when these up-front, inaccurate, high-level estimates get turned prematurely into hard commitments that most projects get into trouble.

Steve McConnell refers to this dysfunctional behavior as the cone of uncertainty (Figure 5, *The cone of uncertainty reminds us of how greatly our estimates can vary at different stages throughout the project*, on page 101), which reminds us that initial estimates can vary by as much as 400 percent at the inception phase of our project.

The simple fact is that *accurate up-front estimates aren't possible*, and we need to stop pretending they are.

The only question our up-front estimates can attempt to answer is this:

IS THIS PROJECT EVEN POSSIBLE !?
(GIVEN THE TIME AND RESOURCES WE'VE GOT)

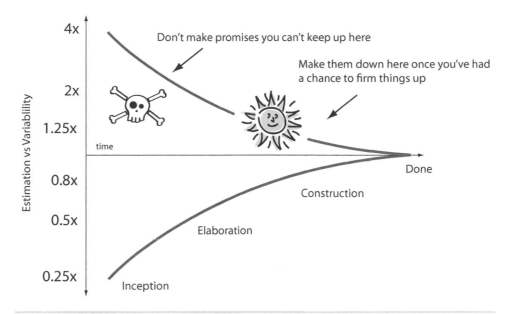

Figure 5—The cone of uncertainty reminds us of how greatly our estimates can vary at different stages throughout the project.

What we need is a way of estimating that does the following:

- Allows us to plan for the future
- Reminds us that our estimates are guesses
- Acknowledges the inherent complexities in creating software

7.2 Turning Lemons into Lemonade

In agile, we accept that our initial, high-level estimates aren't to be trusted. However, we also understand that budgets need to be created and expectations need to be set.

To make that happen, the warrior does what anyone would do who is looking to firm up any estimate. They build something, measure how long that takes, and use that for planning going forward.

For that to work, we need two things:

- Stories that are sized *relatively* to each other
- A *point-based* system to track progress

Let's look at each of these in more detail and see how they help us plan.

Relative Sizing

Imagine you knew it took ten seconds to eat one chocolate chip cookie, and you were asked to estimate how long it would take you to devour a pile of seven and fourteen cookies (glass of milk included). What would you guess?

If it takes 10 secs to eat one of these ...

how long should it take to devour these?

Om nom nom

7 cookies

14 cookies

10 secs

? secs

? secs

Now imagine you were asked to estimate something else—something simple but maybe something you haven't done many times before. How long do you think it would take you do these four simple tasks? (See Figure 6, *Estimating Absolutely*, on page 103.)

If you are like most people, you probably found estimating the cookies relatively easy (pun intended) and the other tasks absolutely harder.

If one cookie = 10 sec
then seven cookies = 10 sec x 7 = 70 sec
and fourteen cookies = 10 sec x 14 = 140 secs

> x2 as big

The difference between the two exercises was that with the cookies we estimated relatively while the card counting we estimated absolutely.

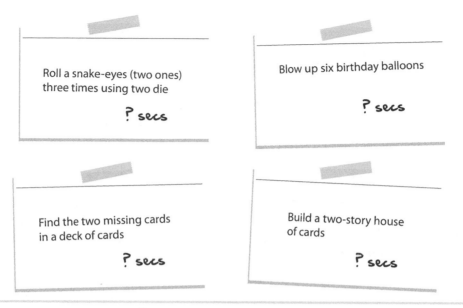

Roll a snake-eyes (two ones) three times using two die

? secs

Blow up six birthday balloons

? secs

Find the two missing cards in a deck of cards

? secs

Build a two-story house of cards

? secs

Figure 6—Estimating Absolutely

Science has shown that estimating relatively is something we humans are actually pretty good at. When you put two rocks in front of us, we can tell quite accurately how much bigger one rock is than the other.

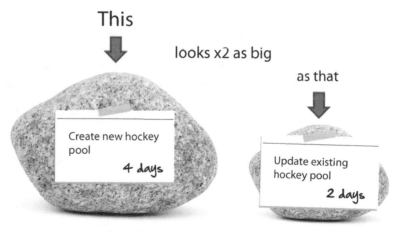

This

looks x2 as big

as that

Create new hockey pool

4 days

Update existing hockey pool

2 days

Where we struggle is with telling you precisely how much bigger it is (estimating absolutely).

This simple principle forms the cornerstone of agile estimation and planning. By sizing our stories relatively to each other and measuring how fast we can go, we have all the ingredients we need to begin forming our agile plan.

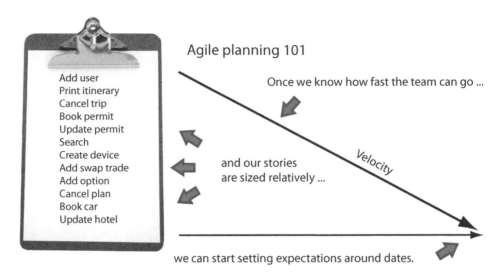

Now, one challenge with estimating relatively is that a single day in our estimates won't always equal one day in our plans. The team will work either slower or faster than we originally estimated.

1 RELATIVE DAY ≠ 1 calendar day

To account for this discrepancy and avoid continuously having to reestimate all our stories, agile does estimation using a point-based system.

Point-Based Systems

Point-based systems enable us to track progress and estimate relatively without having to worry about how our actuals compared with our estimates.

Say, for example, we originally estimated a story to take three days when in reality it ends up taking closer to four.

We could try to adjust all our estimates by 33 percent.

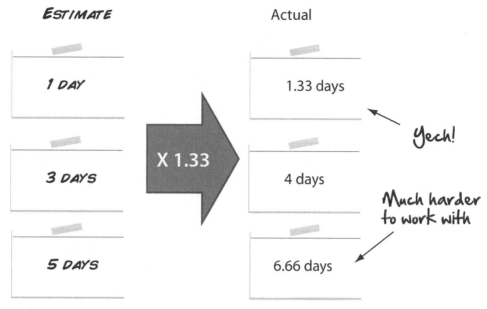

But who wants to work with numbers like 1.33 and 6.66 days? Not only is there a false sense of precision, but what do we do when after delivering a few more stories we find our 1.33 day estimates are closer to 1.66? Readjust again?

To get away from this constant, never-ending rejigging of the numbers, agile recommends freezing your estimates on a simple, easy-to-use point-based system and not tying them to elapsed time on the calendar.

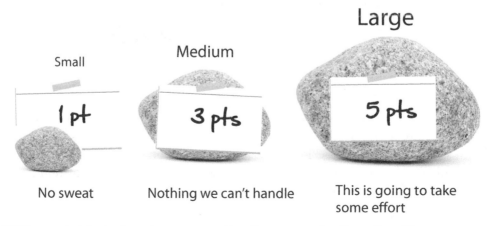

With a point-based system, our units of measure don't matter. The measure is one of relativity—not absoluteness.

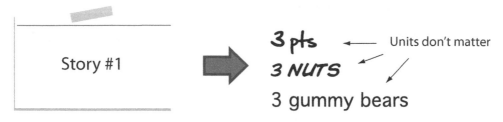

All we are trying to do is capture the *bigness* of a task with a number and size it relatively to all the others. If it helps, you can think of agile estimation as trying to sort your stories according to T-shirt size: small, medium, or large.

Also, as caught up as we tend to get with our estimates, at the end of the day, it doesn't really matter. So long as we size our stories similarly to each other, for every story we over-estimate, there's usually another we under-estimate. So, it all comes out even in the end.

Using a point-based system does the following for us, and studies show we are actually pretty good at it:

- It reminds us that our estimates are guesses.
- It is a measure of pure size (they don't decay over time).
- It's fast, easy, and simple.

You got me. Before we got to agile estimation, whenever the topic of estimation came up, I used the term *days* when really I should have been using *points*. I did this for two reasons. First, we hadn't had a chance to talk about the concept of estimation using *points*. Second, because some agile teams do estimate in days, they just call them something else—ideal days.

Ideal days are just another form of story point. An ideal day is the perfect day where you have no interruptions and are able to work for eight hours straight of uninterrupted bliss.

Of course, we never get ideal days at work, but some teams find the concept useful.

Ideal days can work, but I generally prefer sticking to points. Mostly it's because it makes the fact we are estimating in points explicit, but also because with points I don't have to worry about my ideal day not equaling yours.

For the rest of the book, don't panic if you see points instead of days. I'll stick with points for the remainder of the book, but if you see days, know they are the same thing.

7.3 How Does It Work?

That's enough talk. It's time to get real. Here are two simple estimation techniques you and your team can use to size your stories appropriately for agile planning.

Triangulation

Triangulation is about taking a few sample reference stories and sizing our other stories relatively to these.

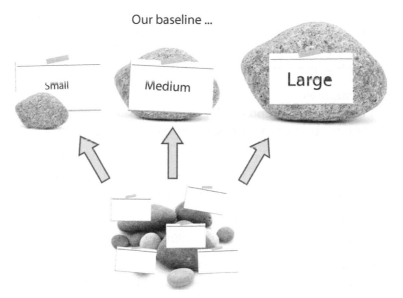

against which we size our remaining stories

Say, for example, there is a local bike shop that just purchased a new inventory system. They've already done their homework and created a good list of user stories. Where they could use some help is in the estimation department.

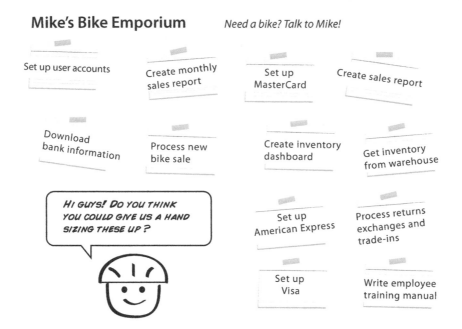

Let's study this list and see whether there are any good candidates that would make good reference stories. Ideally, we would want something small, something medium, and something large enough to fit within one iteration (typically one to two weeks). We could also look for the following:

- Logical groupings
- Stories that go end-to-end (to flesh out the architecture)
- Anything typical of what we'd see throughout the life of the project

These are the kinds of things we want to have in the back of our mind when we are searching for candidate stories. They're just your run-of-the-mill mom-and-pop stories typical of what we'd see while delivering.

After looking at the list, let's say we decide to start with these three as reference stories (Figure 7, *Mike's Bikes baseline*, on page 109).

Now that we have something to compare to, we can go through the rest of the stories and size them up against these candidates (Figure 8, *Mike's Bikes estimated*, on page 109).

Now you may be wondering whether you should ever reestimate your stories. The answer is yes. If you start building some stories and you find out you incorrectly sized a few, absolutely you should resize those outliers and give them a more realistic number.

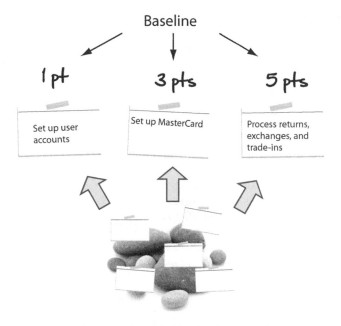

Figure 7—Mike's Bikes baseline

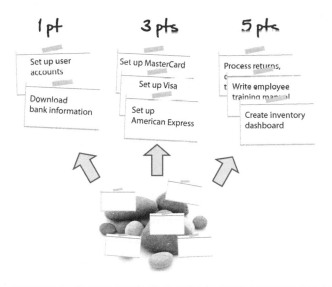

Figure 8—Mike's Bikes estimated

The Wisdom of Crowds

James Surowiecki's *The Wisdom of Crowds.* *[Sur05]* tells this story: in 1906 the British scientist Francis Galton was shocked by the outcome of an experiment he performed at a county fair. Expecting a professional butcher to be able to more accurately guess the weight of a butchered ox, he was surprised and dismayed to find that a crowd of simpletons (with little or no meat-cutting experience) were able not only to guess the final weight of the beast, but they were able to do it within a pound.

This debunked Sir Francis' notion that the experts were always right and would handily outperform a crowd.

When we play planning poker, we similarly look to harness the wisdom of the crowds with regard to our estimates. We are betting that the crowd will be able to come up with a better guess than any one, single individual.

But once you have them correctly sized relatively to each other, it's best to leave them alone. You don't want to be continuously resizing your stories because every time you do, you have to recalibrate your team velocity (which makes planning a little hairier because you will have different velocities for different parts of the plan).

Also, if you ever run into something you've never done before and you don't know how to size it, do a *spike*. A spike is a time-boxed experiment where we do just enough investigation to come up with an estimate and then stop (we don't actually do the story).

Spikes are usually no more than a couple days and are a great way to try something out fast and get just enough information to tell your customer how much it is really going to cost. They can then decide whether it's worth the investment.

Before we wrap up, there is one more handy tool you should know about for doing team-based estimation and building consensus—it's called *planning poker.*

Planning Poker

Planning poker is a game where the development team estimates stories individually first (using a deck of cards with numbers like one, three, and five points on them) and then compares the results collectively together after.

If everyone's estimate is more or less the same, the estimate is kept. If there are differences, however, the team discusses them and estimates again until consensus is reached.

1. Customer reads story.

Development team asks questions

2. Team estimates.

This includes testing.

3. Team discusses.

4. Team estimates again.

Repeat until consensus reached.

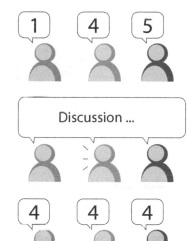

Planning poker works because the people doing the estimating are the ones doing the work. This includes developers, but it could also include DBAs, designers, technical writers, or anyone else responsible for the delivery of the story.

It's powerful because of the discussion. When someone says a story is really small and someone else says it's really big, it doesn't matter who's right or wrong (that will sort itself out). A valuable discussion is about to take place, and that's what matters.

Just to be clear, planning poker isn't a voting system (that is, three juniors don't outvote one experienced senior). But it is a way for people to voice their opinions and ideally arrive at a better estimate for having done so.

And don't be fooled by commercial planning poker decks full of cards with numbers like 8, 13, 20, 40, and 100—you don't need them.

Keep it simple. Size your stories small (one, three, and five points with the occasional epic) and avoid the false sense of precision and noise these other numbers bring.

Master Sensei and the aspiring warrior

STUDENT: *Master, is it true that agile doesn't care about accuracy when estimating and relative sizing is all that counts?*

MASTER: *When estimating, one should always give his best, most accurate estimate possible. Hence, it would be misleading to say agile has no regard for accuracy.*

STUDENT: *So, we should shoot for both accuracy and relativity when estimating stories?*

MASTER: *Yes. Estimate as accurately as you can; just understand that you won't be that accurate. Only once our stories are sized relatively and we have measured our team's rate of productivity will the sun shine and our plans grow firmer.*

STUDENT: *So, I should give my best estimate but spend more time ensuring my stories are sized relatively to each other?*

MASTER: *That is so. A little effort goes a long way when estimating. Do not dwell on the inaccuracy of your estimates. Size stories relatively. Accept them for what they are, and set expectations accordingly.*

STUDENT: *Thank you, Master. I will think about this more.*

What's Next?

Congratulations! By learning how to estimate user stories relatively using a point-based system, you now have everything you need to build your first agile plan.

In agile project planning, we'll go over all the tools you need to forecast, track, and create a project plan you and your customer can believe in.

Then, with your plan in hand and inception deck at your side, we'll be ready to get into the meat and potatoes of delivery—agile project execution.

Turn the page to learn the secrets of agile project planning.

CHAPTER 8

Agile Planning: Dealing with Reality

Get used to it, pretty boy. Murphy's law takes no prisoners when it comes to disrupting the best-laid plans. If you don't have a strategy for dealing with change, your project is going to eat you alive.

In this chapter, you're going to learn how to create plans you can believe in and follow through on commitments you and your team make.

By learning how to plan projects the agile way, you'll sleep easier knowing your plan is always up-to-date, you've set expectations openly and honestly, and change isn't something to be feared but instead used as a competitive advantage.

8.1 The Problems with Static Plans

Has this ever happened to you? Your project starts off beautifully. You have the perfect team. The right technology. The perfect plan. And for the first couple weeks of your project, life couldn't be better. Then out of nowhere...bam!

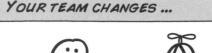

Your lead developer gets poached by another project of great strategic importance (funny, that's what they used to say about yours). "OK, we've got time," you think, "we can handle this." When all of sudden…kapow!

YOU REALIZE YOU AREN'T GOING AS FAST AS YOU'D THOUGHT ...

How you planned it.   **How it's going.**

What you thought your team could do and what they can actually do are two different things. Then, just about halfway through the project…

That simple, easy-to-build web application suddenly looks a lot more daunting and complex. What looked like a slam dunk now looks virtually impossible with the remaining time and resources you have. And then the real bomb goes off.

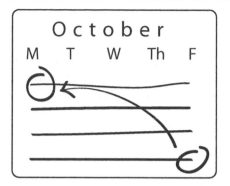

It turns out business needs your application sooner rather than later. In a rush to meet the new deadline, testing gets cut. The team is asked to cancel their vacations. And when it finally does go live, it's of such poor quality nobody can use it. It becomes another late, over-budget, failed IT project.

If this story hits close to home, take comfort—you are not alone. Changing teams, reduced schedules, and ever-shifting requirements are the norm for any interesting software project.

To deal with these realities, we need a way of planning that does the following:

- Delivers great value to our customers
- Is highly visible, open, and honest
- Lets us make promises we can keep
- Enables us to adapt and change the plan when necessary

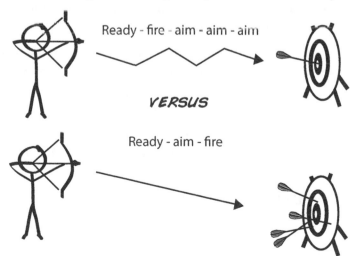

With this context of having to deal with change, let's now take a look at the agile plan.

8.2 Enter the Agile Plan

In its simplest form, agile planning is nothing more than measuring the speed a team can turn user stories into working, production-ready software and then using that to figure out when they'll be done.

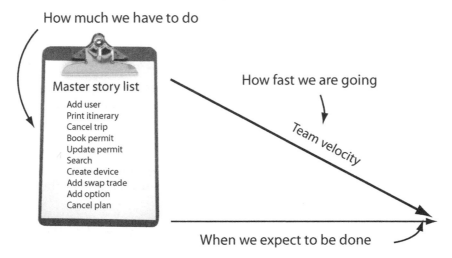

Our to-do list on an agile project is called the *master story list*. It contains a list of all the features our customers would like to see in their software.

The speed at which we turn user stories into working software is called the *team velocity*. It's what we use for measuring our team's productivity and for setting expectations about delivery dates in the future.

The engine for getting things done is the agile *iteration*—one- to two-week sprints of work where we turn user stories into working, production-ready software.

To give us a rough idea about delivery dates, we take the total effort for the project, divide it by our estimated team velocity, and calculate how many iterations we think we'll require to deliver our project. This becomes our project plan.

 # iterations = total effort / estimated team velocity

For example:

 # iterations = 100 pts / 10 pts per iteration = 10 iterations

The One Time I Was Asked to Leave a Project

I was once at a client site where we were trying to build a $2 million gas accounting system for $700,000, and when it became apparent that the budget was about half of what it needed to be, the company started to tighten the screws asking us to work overtime and weekends to get the project "back on schedule."

Well, you can imagine how this went over. Every time we got together during our iteration planning meetings, they would insist we double our current velocity, and we would refuse.

One day it came to a head. They pulled me aside and said that by not signing up for more work, we had just ruined over a year's worth of building credibility with the end customer and that my services would no longer be required on the project.

At the end of the day, I failed that client. To be fair, we made some big mistakes (such as not doing an inception deck in the beginning and not clearly explaining how agile planning worked).

But culture is important, and not everyone likes the visibility and transparency that agile brings. Make sure your customers know how agile planning works going in and where you are going to flex when reality and the plan start to differ.

It's really important to understand that our first project plan isn't a hard commitment. It's a guess. We don't know our team's velocity at the beginning of the project, and until we build something of value and measure how long that takes, we won't know how realistic our dates are looking.

Treating initial plans as hard commitments is what kills projects before they've even started.

Now, as we start delivering, one of two things is going to happen. We are going to discover that a) we are going faster than expected or b) we are going slower than we originally thought (Figure 9, *Faster or slower than expect*, on page 118).

Faster than expected means you and your team are ahead of schedule. Slower than expected (more the norm) means you have too much to do and not enough time.

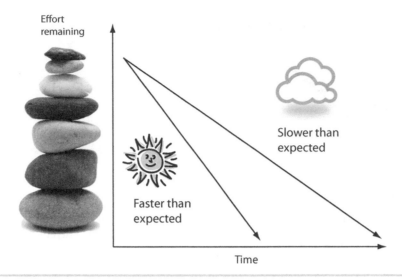

Figure 9—Faster or slower than expect

When faced with too much to do, agile teams will do less (kind of like what you and I do when faced with a really busy weekend). Instead of sticking with the original plan, they will change it, usually by reducing scope.

8.3 Be Flexible About Scope

Being flexible around scope is how agile projects maintain the integrity of their plans.

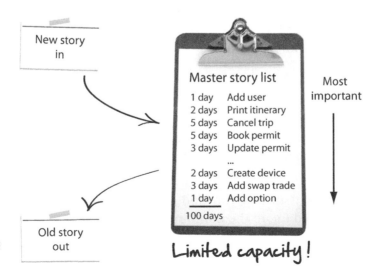

By insisting their customers drop an old story every time a new one comes in, agile teams work within the means of their projects while giving their customers the ability to change their minds (without paying an exorbitant price).

Agile principle

Welcome changing requirements, even late in development. Agile processes harness change for the customer's competitive advantage.

This gets customers away from the notion that they have to throw in the kitchen sink with gathering requirements (less waste), and it lets them and the team learn as they go instead of trying to get everything perfectly right up front.

Now technically speaking, the customer doesn't always have to drop an old story when a new story comes in. For example, if it's a feature they really want and are prepared to pay for it, they could push out the date.

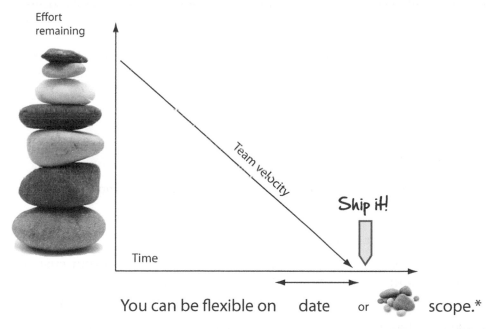

You can be flexible on date or scope.*

* Recommended

What customers can't do, however, is add something to the list and not expect something of equal size to come off. That's wishful thinking, and there is no place for that in agile planning.

When it comes to pushing out the date or being flexible about scope, agilists generally prefer the latter. Perpetually pushing out release dates is something our industry is unfortunately really good at. What we aren't good at is shipping working software on time.

But regardless of whether you are delivering to a fixed date or working to a core set of features, being flexible about scope is a concept you and your customer need to start getting very good at to keep your plans real and your teams from biting off more than they can chew.

Now you may be wondering what to do if your customer refuses to be flexible about scope, while insisting that you and the team take on more work.

You have a couple of options here.

First, you could perpetuate the lie, turn a blind eye, and continue to follow the old plan just like everyone else. Or you could give overly optimistic estimates, pad your numbers, ignore your team velocity, and hope and pray that things will turn out in the end (often referred to as management by miracle).

Or, when all else fails, you could present the facts as they are, tell it like it is, and then sit and wait in that awkward silence until they realize that you aren't going to cave. You aren't going to continue the facade, and you aren't going to be a willing accomplice in what has been one of the greatest lies our industry has perpetuated over the past 40 years. No one said being a samurai was easy.

Now let's take a look at how to build your first agile plan.

8.4 Your First Plan

Creating your first agile plan isn't all that much different from preparing for a busy weekend. It all starts with a good list.

Step 1: Create Your Master Story List

The master story list is a collection of user stories (features) your customer is going to want to see in their software. It is prioritized by your customers, it is estimated by your team, and it forms the basis of your project plan.

A good master story list will usually have about one to six months worth of work. There is no point tracking stories much beyond that because a) you don't know what the world will look like six months from now and b) you'll probably never get to them anyway, so why bother?

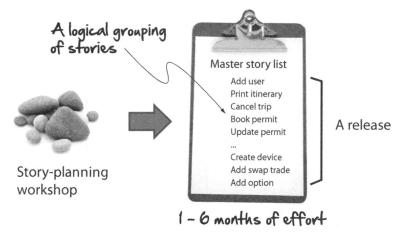

A logical grouping of stories

Story-planning workshop

Master story list

Add user
Print itinerary
Cancel trip
Book permit
Update permit
...
Create device
Add swap trade
Add option

A release

1 – 6 months of effort

Now sometimes you'll deliver everything on your list, but more likely you won't because there is always more to do than time and money allow.

So, to set expectations around what is in and what is out of scope, agile teams will take a subset of stories from the master story list and refer to them as a *release*.

Define Your Release

A release is a logical grouping of stories that makes sense to your customer —something worth bundling up and deploying. It's also sometimes referred to as a *minimal marketable feature set* (or MMF[1]).

The first *M* in MMF, minimal, is there to remind us that we want to start delivering value fast (and that 80 percent of a system's value often comes from a mere 20 percent of its features). So, you want to choose the fewest number of features that deliver the most value in the first release of your software.

Agile principle

Simplicity—the art of maximizing the amount of work not done—is essential.

The second *M*, marketable, reminds us that whatever we release needs to be of value to our customer (or else they'll never use it). So, minimal and marketable are two key drivers when choosing candidate stories for your first release.

---

1. *Software by Numbers: Low-Risk, High-Return Development [DC03]*

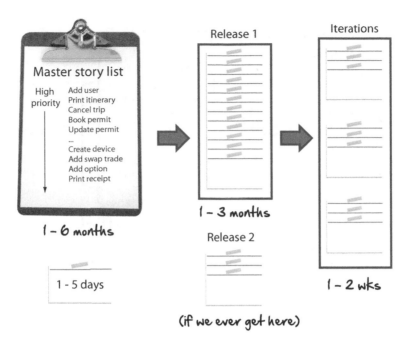

Once you have your release and master story list defined, the next thing you need to do is size things up.

Step 2: Size It Up

In Chapter 7, *Estimation: The Fine Art of Guessing*, on page 99, we saw how teams can use agile estimation techniques to size stories up.

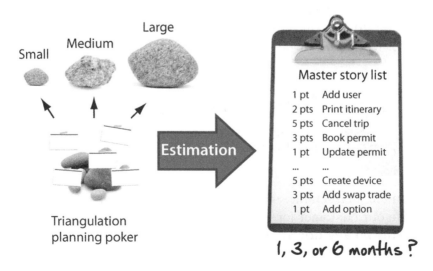

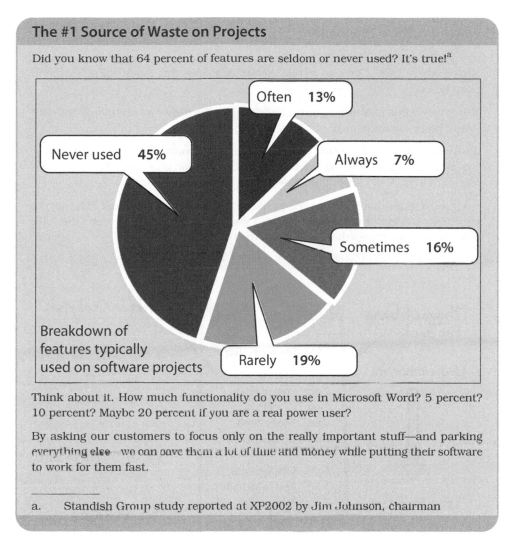

The #1 Source of Waste on Projects

Did you know that 64 percent of features are seldom or never used? It's true![a]

Often **13%**

Never used **45%**

Always **7%**

Sometimes **16%**

Breakdown of features typically used on software projects

Rarely **19%**

Think about it. How much functionality do you use in Microsoft Word? 5 percent? 10 percent? Maybe 20 percent if you are a real power user?

By asking our customers to focus only on the really important stuff—and parking everything else—we can save them a lot of time and money while putting their software to work for them fast.

a.   Standish Group study reported at XP2002 by Jim Johnson, chairman

Here you want to get a sense of how big this thing is and whether you are looking at a one-, three-, six-, or nine-month journey.

Once your to-do list is sized, you're ready to talk priorities.

Step 3: Prioritize

Lightning could strike at any moment (meaning the project could be canceled or shortened), so we gotta get the important stuff in first. Having your customer prioritize the master story list from a business point of view ensures they'll get the biggest bang for their buck.

Velocity—It's a Team Thing!

When we create plans based on our team's velocity, we are making a commitment as a team. We're saying, "We as a team feel we do deliver this much value, each and every iteration."

This is very different from measuring individual productivity—which leads to the dark side of project management.

If you want more bugs, more rework, more miscommunication, less collaboration, less skill, and less knowledge sharing, then by all means, promote, highlight, and reward individual developer productivity.

Just understand that by doing so, you are killing the very spirit and behavior we want to foster and promote on our projects: sharing ideas, helping each other out, and watching for things that fall through the cracks.

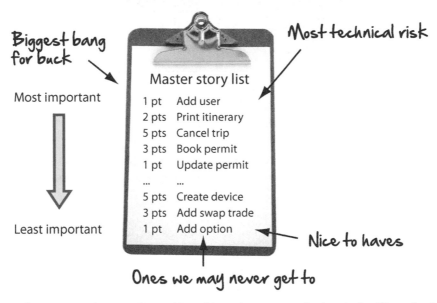

Although your customers have the ultimate say in what gets built and when, you also have a duty to make suggestions about what stories would be good candidates to build in the beginning to reduce architectural risk.

For example, good candidate stories to tackle early are those that are important to the customer and prove the architecture. By connecting the dots early and going end-to-end, you can eliminate a lot of risk while gaining invaluable insight into how to best build the system. So, don't be afraid to speak up—your expertise and experience matter.

With our prioritized, estimated list in hand, we are almost ready to start talking dates. But before you can do that, you need to guess how fast you and your team can go.

Step 4: Estimate Your Team's Velocity

Agile plans work because we plan for the future based on what we've proven we could deliver in the past. And since we don't know how fast our team can go at the start of a project, we have to guess.

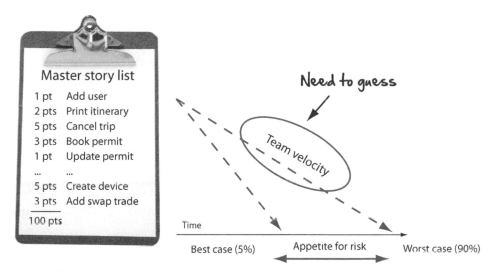

Now if all your stories were the same size, then this would be one simplified way of looking at it:

Team velocity = stories completed/iteration

More often than not, however, our stories will vary by size, in which case team velocity is usually this:

Team velocity = story pts completed / iteration

Now in the beginning of your project, your velocity is going to fluctuate, so don't panic. This is normal while your team sorts themselves out and figures out best how to work together. But after three or four iterations, your velocity should start to settle down, and you'll start to get an idea of how fast your team can go (Figure 10, *Velocity will fluctuate*, on page 126).

There are no hard-and-fast rules on how to estimate your team's velocity. Ask your team what they think they can get done per iteration, and be sure to take things into account like availability to customer and whether your team is co-located.

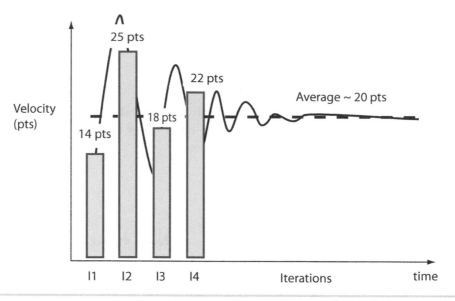

Figure 10—Velocity will fluctuate

Also remind the team what the definition of done is (Section 1.3, *Done Means Done*, on page 8) and that delivering a story in agile means analysis, testing, design, and coding. The whole thing.

It's also best to not be too aggressive in your initial estimate. The secret to happiness is lowered expectations, and if you shoot too high, you are going to have a harder conversation than if you shoot too low. So, be conservative, remind your stakeholders that it's a guess, and start measuring from day one.

With our list in hand and our velocity estimated, we are now in a good place to start setting expectations around dates.

Step 5: Pick Some Dates

You have two options for setting expectations around dates. You can *deliver by date* or you can *deliver by feature set*.

Deliver by Date

Delivery by date is about drawing a line in the sand and saying, "We are going to ship product on this date no matter what."

When new important user stories are discovered, then older, less important ones of equal size come off.

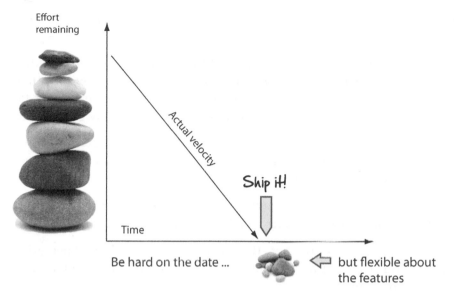

Effort remaining

Actual velocity

Ship it!

Time

Be hard on the date ... but flexible about the features

It forces the tough decision and trade-offs up front (around things such as scope) while creating just enough urgency to let everyone know we gotta get going.

If you can be flexible about the date and are more concerned about a core set of features, you can also *deliver by feature set*.

Deliver by Feature Set

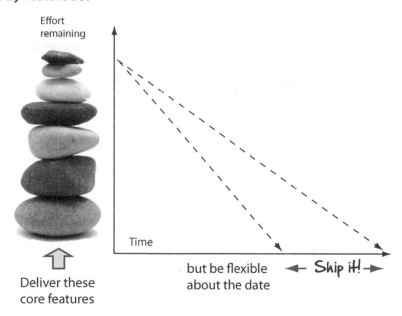

Effort remaining

Time

Deliver these core features

but be flexible about the date

← Ship it! →

This is about picking a core set of features and working on them until they are done.

Being flexible about scope is still part of the equation (as you are still going to discover new features along the way), but the spirit here is that there are a few big rocks the team needs to deliver, and you are prepared to be flexible about the date to make sure those core features collectively get shipped.

The advantage of delivery by feature set is you get your core set of features and the cost of accepting some risk around the date. How much risk is a decision for your customers and sponsors to make.

And that is how you create an agile plan! You create a estimated, prioritized master story list, estimate your team's velocity, and pick your date.

Before we go too much further, there is one more excellent expectation setting–tool you need to know about before we leave the art of agile planning: the burn-down chart.

8.5   The Burn-Down Chart

Although we haven't formally introduced the project burn-down chart, we've seen glimpses of it on our travels. It's the graph that shows how quickly we as a team are burning through our customer's user stories, and it tells us when we can expect to be done.

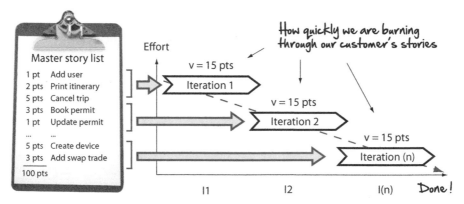

On the y-axis we track the amount of work remaining (days of effort or points), and on the x-axis we track time by iteration. Simply record the amount of work (pts) remaining each iteration, and plot that on the graph. The slope of the line is the team velocity (how much the team got done each iteration).

The burn-down chart is a great vehicle for showing the state of your project. With nothing more than a glance you can tell the following:

- How much work has been done
- How much work remains
- The team's velocity
- Our expected completion date

Each column (iteration) on the chart represents the amount of work remaining in the project. We are done when the column burns down to nothing.

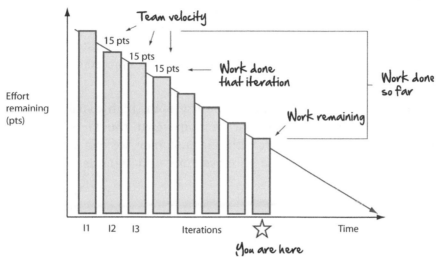

Now, in a perfect world, our velocity would be constant. It would start at 15 pts, gently descend from left to right, and stay there for the duration of the project. In reality, however, our burn-down charts usually look a lot more like this:

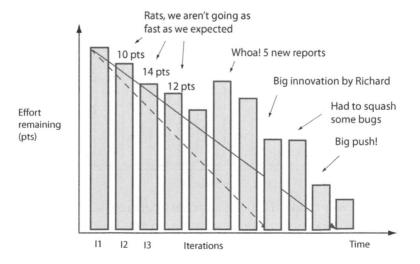

Things don't go according to plan. Our team's velocity fluctuates. New stories get discovered. Old stories get dropped.

The burn-down chart makes all these events in your project visible. If the customer decides to add scope to the project, you can instantly see the impact that will have on your delivery date. If the team is slowing down because you lost a valuable team member, that will show up as a drop in team velocity too.

Burn-down charts also tell the story behind the numbers. When something shows up on our burn-down chart, it can help us facilitate a conversation with our stakeholders around things that happen to projects and the impact of decisions that get made.

Project burn-down charts tell it like it is. This is the highly visible part of agile planning. We don't hide anything or sugar-coat the facts. By regularly reviewing the burn-down chart with our customer, we can set expectations openly and honestly and make sure everyone understands when we expect to be done.

The Burn-Up Chart

Another popular form of the burn-down chart is the burn-up chart. It's the same chart, only flipped.

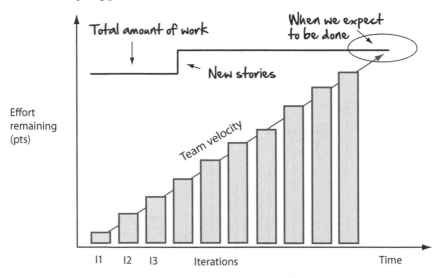

Some people prefer using the burn-up chart because of the way it presents the discovery of new stories. By drawing a steady line across the top, any increase in scope is immediately seen, and it's a bit easier to track over time.

If you like the scope visibility of the burn-up but prefer the simplicity and concept of burning down, you can combine the two. Simply track the total work down each iteration on the burn-down along with the work remaining.

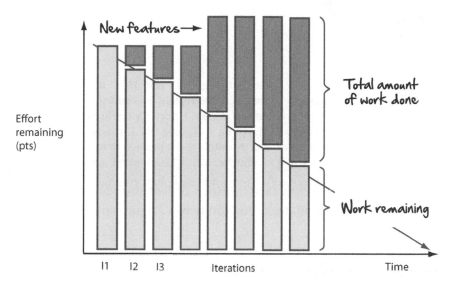

Burn-up or burn-down chart—it's totally up to you. Just make sure you have an easy, visible way to set expectations around how much work is remaining and when you expect to be done.

8.6 Transitioning a Project to Agile

There are lots of ways to transition to agile if you're already mid-project. You're probably thinking about doing this because:

a) what you are currently doing isn't working, or
b) you need to get something out the door fast.

If your problem is one of alignment, create an inception deck (Chapter 3, *How to Get Everyone on the Bus*, on page 35).

Ignorance Was Bliss

I remember once asking a VP what he thought of agile. He said, "It's a love-hate relationship." On one hand, he loved the visibility agile brought to a project. But he also hated the visibility agile brought to a project. Before, he could just bury his head in the sand and at least pretend everything was going OK. But now it's there. Every day. Staring him right in the face. The true state of the project. It served as a constant reminder of how much they had to improve, which he admitted was a good thing.

You may not need a full-on deck, but you need to make sure everyone knows the following:

- Why you are there
- What you are trying to accomplish
- Who's the customer
- What big rocks you need to move
- Who's calling the shots

If there is any doubt about these or any other of the inception deck questions, play the appropriate inception deck card, ask the tough questions, and get some alignment.

If you have to ship something fast, throw out the current plan, and create a new one you can believe in. Just as if you are creating a new agile plan from scratch, create a to-do list, size things up, set some priorities, and deliver the minimal amount of functionality to get something out the door.

If you need to show progress but have to work within the confines of your original plan, start delivering something of value every week. Take one or two valuable features each week and just do them—completely. Once you've shown you can deliver (and regained an element of trust), slowly rework the plan and define a release based on your now measured team velocity and how much work there is remaining. Then simply keep delivering until you have something you can ship. Update the plan as you go, execute fiercely, and use the sense of urgency you've been given to blow through anything standing in your way.

Let's see what some of this stuff looks like practice.

8.7   Putting It into Practice

We've done the heavy lifting. You now know all the theory. Let's put the theory into practice and revisit the four challenges we faced at the beginning of the chapter and see how we could handle them with our new agile plan.

Scenario #1: Your Customer Discovers Some New Requirements

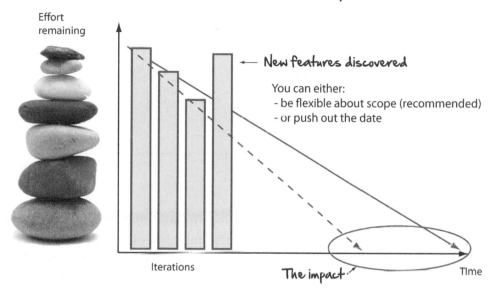

When your customer discovers what they really want in their software, ask them how they'd like to handle it. You can push out the release date (which is like saying we are going to need more money), or you can drop some of the less important stories (preferred).

Don't get emotional when you have this conversation. It's not your call to make. You are simply the vessel for communicating that which is and can be completely impartial toward the outcome. Your responsibility is to make them aware of the impact of their decisions and give them the information they need to make an informed decision.

If your customer really wants it all, create a nice-to-have list and tell them that if there is time at the end of the project, these are the first stories you'll tackle. But make it clear. The nice-to-haves are currently off the table and aren't part of the core plan.

Scenario #2: You Aren't Going as Fast as You'd Hoped

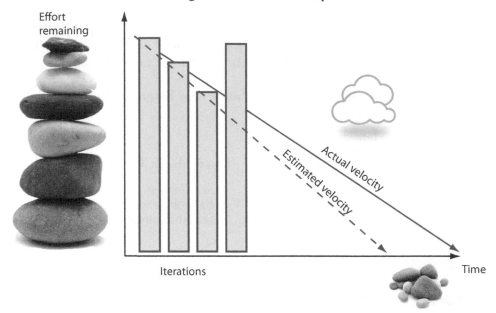

If after three or four iterations you notice your velocity isn't where you had hoped it would be, don't panic. We knew this might happen, which is why we set expectations accordingly and told our customer not to trust our initial plans. The good news is that we know about it now and can adjust course as necessary.

Being flexible about scope is the preferred method for restoring balance. You can also look at adding resources (this will initially slow you down) or pushing out the date (both less than ideal).

The important thing is to have the conversation and give your customer some options. Yes, this may make you uncomfortable, but you can't hide this stuff. Bad news early is the agile way.

Now, we are not completely defenseless when it comes to figuring out whether we have enough time. There is one strategy for ensuring that when you do have the "too much to do, not enough time" conversation, you are coming at it from a place of complete honesty, transparency, and integrity.

The Way of the Spartan Warrior

The way of the Spartan warrior is based on a simple premise. If we can't deliver a stripped-down, minimalist version of the application with the time and resources we've got, then the plan is clearly wrong and needs to change.

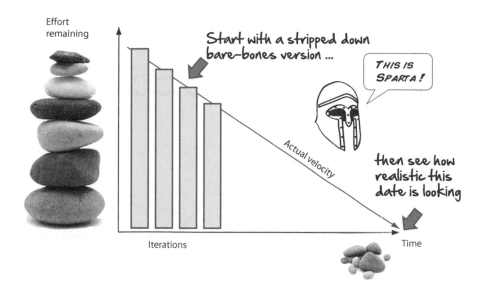

It works like this: take one or two really important features for your project (something core that goes from end to end through your entire architecture), and measure how long it takes to build a stripped-down, bare-bones, minimalistic version of those features.

Then use that against your remaining relatively sized stories to see whether a minimalistic version of the application is even possible with the time and resources you have.

If your dates are looking good, right on! Keep on truckin'.

If your dates are looking bad, great! At least you know about it now.

Going Spartan lets you have the "we need to change the plan" conversation from a place of strength and integrity. It's not based on wishful thinking. There's no need to get emotional. It's just the facts. It's better to know this now than later.

And with this information, you and your customer can now have a real discussion about what features to go Spartan on and which ones might need a little more spit and polish. Then you can tune your project plan to deliver the greatest bang for your buck, all while working within your means.

Scenario #3: You Lose a Valuable Team Member

Gauging the impact of losing a valuable team member is never easy. You know you are going to take a hit; it's just hard to say how much.

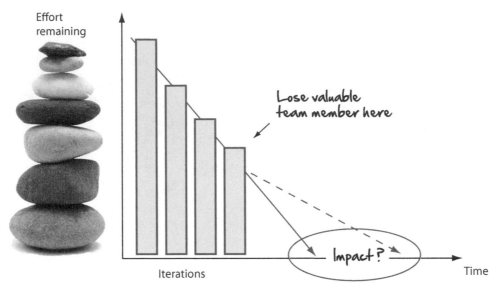

When it comes to setting expectations around changing team members, you don't need to get too scientific. Just tell your customer that the project is obviously going to take a hit (guess if you can), and once you've had a chance to measure the impact through your team velocity (two or three iterations), you'll be able to tell them exactly how much.

Of course, your manager might turn around and say the new person they've hired is every bit as good (even better) than the teammate you are losing and you shouldn't experience any loss of velocity.

Maybe. But don't count on it. The new person may not fit in. Or they may have bluffed their way through the interview process with a great resume and a firm handshake. Believe it when you see it. Until then, be skeptical and set expectations accordingly.

Scenario #4: You Run Out of Time

The textbook answer here is to be flexible about scope. If you halve the schedule, you gotta halve the number of features you want delivered. It's that simple.

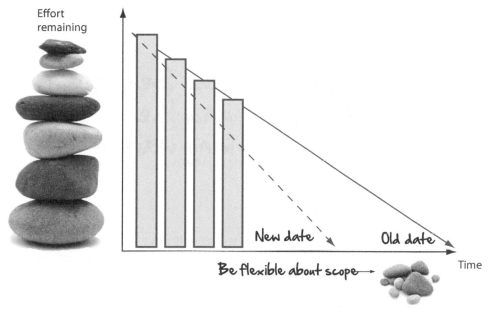

The nontextbook answer, however, is to sit down with your customer and to look for innovative ways to help them.

Maybe there are some stories that can be delivered in a stripped-down or Spartan state. Or maybe twenty static reports can be replaced with one really good dynamic one.

Helping them out in their time of need will go a long way to building the kind of relationship you want with your customer. You want to be seen as a trusted advisor, and one way of doing that is to give them options.

Just don't be strong-armed or bullied into committing to something you and the team can't deliver. That's not doing anyone any favors. And this collaboration thing has to be two-way. Just be honest, and tell them what it's going to take.

Master Sensei would now like to spend a round with you in the agile dojo to see what you have learned.

Master Sensei and the aspiring warrior

Welcome, student. I am glad to see you are still alive. Here I would like to take you through a real-world scenario one of our students recently experienced in the field of battle.

Scenario: Everything is fixed on the project, and there is no ability to change the plan.

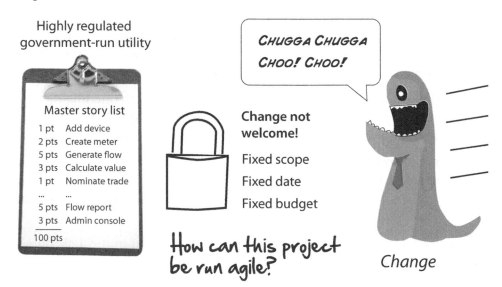

MASTER: *This project is for a large government agency. Because they are spending taxpayers' money, they are closely audited and can't afford anything in the way of change with regard to scope, cost, and deadlines. Everything is fixed. Should this project consider using agile as a means of delivery?*

STUDENT: *If the scope, date, and budget are truly fixed and they are not able to update or change the plan, I don't see how agile can be used in this situation, Master.*

MASTER: Is that so? When projects try to fix time, budget, scope, and quality, they soon discover that these Furious Four cannot be contained. Something must always give, because change is ever-present. Their only choice is whether they want to make the change visible or hide it.

STUDENT: But how can one make the change visible and yet comply with the mandate of no change?

MASTER: This is where the warrior must use all of her experience and skill. What if the creation of a parking lot for old stories that were no longer in scope were sufficient for the auditors to trace what changes had occurred on the project? This would give them the traceability to show differences between the original and actual plan, while losing none of the plan's original integrity.

STUDENT: So, Master, you are saying that regardless of whether they like it or not, the plan is going to change.

MASTER: Hai.

STUDENT: And that by simply documenting the changes, they may be able to meet the requirements of the auditor, while building a system that meets the needs of their customers.

MASTER: That is so.

STUDENT: Thank you, Master. I will meditate on this more.

Lesson: Change will always be there. Sometimes we just need to be creative in how we present and manage it.

What's Next?

Well done, mon ami! You've survived the inception deck. You've mastered the art and science of user stories and estimation. And you've now learned how to bring it all together in the agile plan.

You are now ready for the next leg of your journey—agile project execution. Here you are going to learn how to turn those good intentions and plans into something real—working, tested, production-ready software.

And it all begins with the humble iteration.

Part IV

Agile Project Execution

CHAPTER 9

Iteration Management: Making It Happen

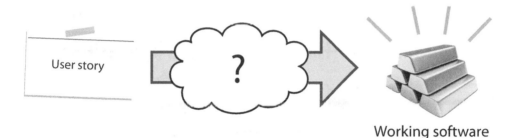

User story

Working software

Welcome to Part IV, "Agile Project Execution." Here we take the plans we created in Parts II and III and turn those good intentions into something our customers can use—working software.

In this chapter on iteration management, I am going to take you behind the scenes and show you how agile projects get things done through the power of the iteration.

Afterwards, in Chapter 10, *Creating an Agile Communication Plan*, on page 161, you'll see how a typical agile iteration works and the various meetings and sync points agile teams use to keep it all moving, and in Chapter 11, *Setting Up a Visual Workspace*, on page 173, you'll find out how making a few simple changes to your workspace will enable you to work with even greater clarity and focus.

9.1 How to Deliver Something of Value Every Week

So, you have the plan. You know why you are here, and you are ready to execute. Now what? How do you turn an index card with a few words scribbled on it into production-ready, working software?

Well, first, you won't have time to write everything down. You are going to need a way of doing analysis that is light, that is accurate, and that gives exactly what you need, just when you need it.

Second, your development practices will need to be rock-solid. We won't have time to continuously go back and fix buggy code. It has to work out of the gate. That means well-designed, well-tested, completely integrated code as you go.

Third, your testing will have to be lockstep with development. You can't afford to wait until the end of the project to see whether everything works. You are going to have to maintain the health and integrity of the system from day one of the project.

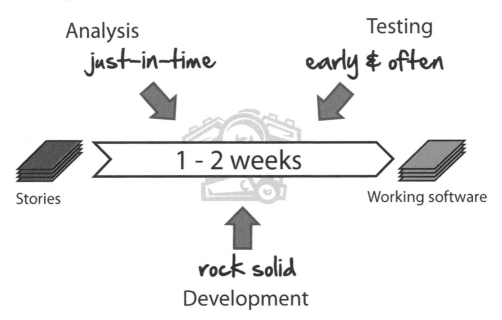

But if you could do these three things, you might just be able to produce something of value every week. And one great, disciplined way to do that is to make use of the agile iteration.

9.2 The Agile Iteration

By now you probably have a pretty good idea of what an agile iteration looks like. It's that time-boxed (one- to two-week) period where we take our customers' top stories and convert them into working software.

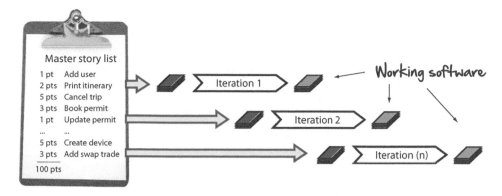

It's your engine for getting stuff done on an agile project. The goal is to produce something of value every time we turn the crank. That means whatever it takes to produce working, tested software needs to happen during an iteration.

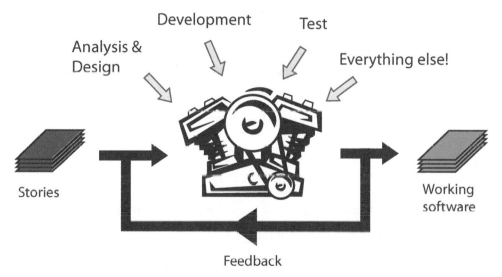

Iterations also enable us to adjust course when necessary. If our priorities change or reality does something unexpected, we can adjust course at the end of each iteration. We usually don't change stories mid-iteration (because that would be too disruptive for the team). But as you'll see shortly in Chapter 10, *Creating an Agile Communication Plan*, on page 161, the opportunity to refocus is there if you need it.

But enough talk. The best way to see how an iteration works is to see it in action. Let's now take a user story and see what it takes to turn it into production-ready, working software.

9.3 Help Wanted

Help! The start date for BigCo's construction project has just been moved up a month, and our good friend Mr. Kelly needs a website his contractors can access to create construction safety work permits.

We obviously won't have time to build the entire website in a single iteration, but Mr. Kelly would really appreciate it if we could deliver these two stories in the next two weeks.

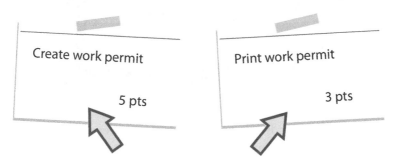

To make that happen, there are three steps all user stories go through when getting converted into working software:

1. Analysis and design (making the work ready)
2. Development (doing the work)
3. Testing (checking the work)

Let's now take a closer look and see what's involved in each of these steps.

9.4   Step 1: Analysis and Design: Making the Work Ready

There are two key concepts to agile analysis: just-enough and just-in-time. Just-enough analysis is about doing whatever it takes to make the work ready —nothing more, nothing less.

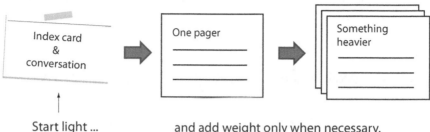

A small, co-located team, with an on-site customer, isn't going to need a lot in the way of formal documentation. A card and a conversation (backed by a few well chosen diagrams and pictures) are often enough.

A medium-sized team that's a little more spread out (but still walking distance from each other) might need a little more. A one pager with a short description, a task breakdown, and a list of test criteria might be better suited for them.

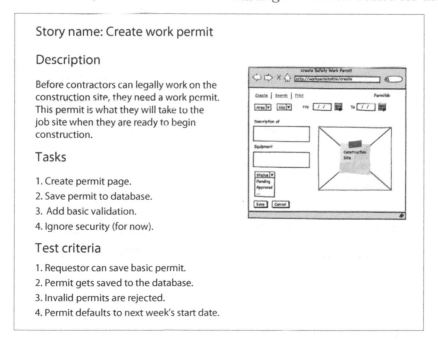

A really large project, with a distributed team living in Chicago, London, and Singapore, will obviously need something more to keep everyone aligned and headed in the right direction.

The point is there is no one right level of detail for agile analysis. There is only what is right for you and your project.

You can always add weight later if you need it, but carrying any unnecessary extra baggage is only going to slow you down. So, start light and add weight if and when you need it.

The other pillar of agile analysis is just-in-time.

Just-in-time analysis is about doing the deep-dive analysis on your user story just before you need it (usually the iteration before).

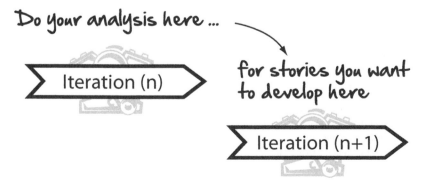

We don't know what the world is going to look like a month from now. Things change. So, sprinting ahead and trying to get everything right up front usually ends up being a big waste. Instead, you want to hold off on doing the deep-dive analysis on a story until the last possible moment—just before you need it.

Doing it this way ensures the following:

- Analysis gets done with the latest and greatest information.
- You and your customer give yourself a chance to learn and innovate as you go.
- You avoid having to do a lot of rework.

If what you are doing is really complex and requires more time, take it. Do whatever it takes to make the work ready. Just don't go so far ahead that you end up having to throw it all away because of how much things have changed.

So, what would the analysis artifacts look like for a story like "Create work permit"?

Well, there's nothing like a good flowchart to kick things off.

Start with a good flowchart

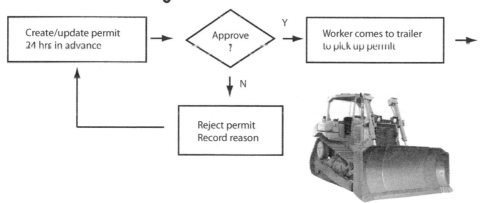

Flowcharts are great because in a simple, visible way, they show how systems work, they show the steps people need to go through, and they can be annotated to show just about anything you need to capture from a process flow point of view.

You can then gain some insight and understanding into who the users of your system are and what they are trying to do with *personas*.

Then create some personas

Administrator

"Amanda"

Needs to be able to add and remove users to the system.

Is comfortable with computers.

Runs the office (all permits are distributed through her for new construction workers).

Requestor

"Robert"

Construction manager or engineer who will request permits on behalf of his/her employees.

WIll know details about the work.

Responsible for ensuring permits are requested on time.

Approver

"Mr. Kelly"

Safety and loss management officer responsible for overall safety at construction site.

Must approve any permits before being issued.

Final word on validity of permit.

Personas are simple descriptions or stereotypes for the roles different people will play when they use your software. They help bring some personality to the system. These are real people, with real problems, and understanding where they are coming from will help you meet their needs.

Try different designs fast using paper prototypes

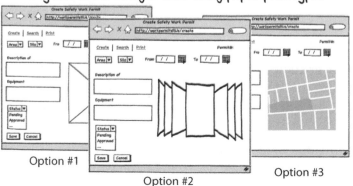

Option #1

Option #2

Option #3

Then when it comes to actual design, the world is our oyster! Instead of just latching onto the first design you think of, rapidly prototype a number of different designs and options quickly with cheap, inexpensive paper prototypes.

The nice thing about getting your team together and collaborating on paper is you almost always end up with something better than what any one person would come up with on their own.

Once you've worked out a design, you can then sit down with your customer and write out some test criteria and be really clear on what success for this story looks like.

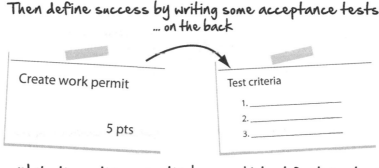

This is where you sit down with your customer and ask, "How are we going to know when this thing is working?"

You can go into as much or as little detail here as you want. You can start high level and just make sure the team understands what major pieces of functionality need to work for the story to be a success.

Or, if your story is very technical in nature and has a lot of business rules and details, you may need to spend more time and write those out too (even better if you can eventually capture those in some form of automated test).

Are there other tools and techniques we could be using for analysis? For sure! Storyboards, concurrency diagrams, process maps, wireframes, and all the other useful analysis and user experience techniques known to man are at your disposal (for other analysis ideas, see Section 6.4, *How to Host a Story-Gathering Workshop*, on page 93).

Remember, no one went to school to be taught how to do this stuff. Be creative. There is no one right way.

Oh yeah, and if you're wondering what happened to the print story, it turned out we didn't need it. Printing the permit through the browser will be good enough for the first release, so we dropped it. Good thing we didn't waste any time on the analysis!

With our analysis done, we're now ready to do the work.

9.5 Step 2: Development: Do the Work

Here we take our just-in-time analysis and convert it into pure gold—or in our case, production-ready working software.

Now production-ready software, like gold, doesn't come for free. It takes hard work, great discipline, and technical excellence.

For example, on agile projects there are certain things we need to do:

- We need to write automated tests.
- We need to continuously evolve and improve our designs.
- We need to continuously integrate our code to produce working software.
- We need to make sure the code matches the language our customers use when they talk about the system.

We don't have the time or space to cover every good software engineering practice out there, but what we are going to cover are those I like to call the *non-negotiables* (or the ones you'd be crazy to go without).

In future chapters, such as Chapter 12, *Unit Testing: Knowing It Works*, on page 185; Chapter 13, *Refactoring: Paying Down Your Technical Debt*, on page 195; Chapter 14, *Test-Driven Development*, on page 207; as well as Chapter 15, *Continuous Integration: Making It Production-Ready*, on page 217, we will cover refactoring, TDD, and continuous integration in great detail and show how they all work to produce production-ready code.

Step 2: Development: Do the Work • 153

What About Pair Programming?

Few agile/XP practices have attracted more attention and controversy than this one.

Pair programming is the act of two programmers sitting down at one computer and working together on a story.

Seeing two valuable resources sitting down at one computer would understandably make any manager nervous. They think their team's productivity has just been halved, and that would be true if programming were merely typing.

But it's not. And one good idea or innovation can often save teams a ton of work and rework later. With pairing you spread valuable knowledge and practices throughout the team, you catch more bugs early, and you increase code quality by having two people reviewing every line of code.

It's not for everyone, and you have to respect how people work. But if your team is open to pairing (this applies to analysis and testing too), it can often more than pay for itself in return.

For now just appreciate that none of this agile magic happens unless it is backed by some hard-core software engineering work behind the scenes.

Let's now take a look at a special case iteration for your project—the first one (or what is otherwise known as iteration 0).

Setting Things Up with Iteration 0

Depending on how you look at it, iteration 0 is your first iteration, or it's the iteration before you really start. It's about setup.

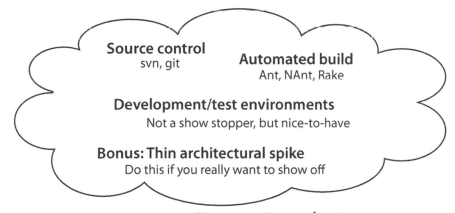

Source control
svn, git

Automated build
Ant, NAnt, Rake

Development/test environments
Not a show stopper, but nice-to-have

Bonus: Thin architectural spike
Do this if you really want to show off

Things we usually need to do before we can really get going on our stories

If we were mid-project, we would normally just dive in and start doing the work on a given story after doing the analysis. But if we are just starting a new project, there are certain things we'd like to have in place before we begin our work. We call this setup phase *iteration 0*.

Iteration 0 is about getting our house in order. It's about setting up things such as version control, creating our automated build, and getting our development and test (and if we can, production) environments working so we have something to deploy against.

If you really want to show off, slip in a basic version of one of the upcoming stories (something that goes end-to-end and tests the architecture).

Once the development work is done, we are almost there. All we need to do now is check the work.

9.6   Step 3: Test: Check the Work

Now it would be pretty embarrassing if we did all this heavy lifting and then didn't follow through to make sure everything worked. Checking the work is where we make sure our work is up to snuff while getting some feedback from our customer.

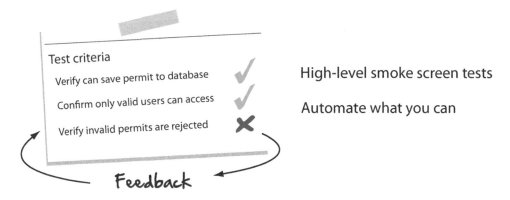

Walking the test criteria while demoing your software to your customer is one good way to show them it works. It's even better if you can get your customer to drive through the demo while you sit back and observe how *they* use the software.

Now I know what you're thinking. With all the testing that goes on with an agile project, do we even need a formal user acceptance test (UAT) as we get ready to go into production? And the answer is yes, you do. Here's why.

Collective Code Ownership

Nobody owns the code on an agile project. It belongs to the team. That means anyone, at any time, is expected and encouraged to make any changes necessary to complete the work they are doing.

XP calls this practice *collective code ownership*, and it is how agile projects promote communication, consistent architecture, and coding standards across the code base.

Your goal as an agile developer (meaning anyone on the development team) is to make UAT a nonevent. That is, you do such a good job of testing, and getting feedback from the customer during delivery, that when UAT does finally roll around, people really struggle to find anything wrong with the system.

Few teams reach this level of quality the first time around (many never do). So, my advice is to keep your UAT around until you can prove to yourself and your sponsors that you and the team can write code of such quality that a formal, full-blown UAT is no longer required. Until then, keep it.

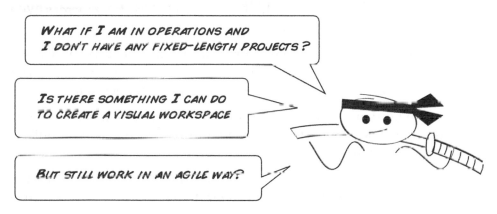

WHAT IF I AM IN OPERATIONS AND I DON'T HAVE ANY FIXED-LENGTH PROJECTS?

IS THERE SOMETHING I CAN DO TO CREATE A VISUAL WORKSPACE

BUT STILL WORK IN AN AGILE WAY?

Absolutely. There is a style of agile better suited for this kind of operation/support style of work. It's a flavor of agile called Kanban.

9.7 Kanban

Kanban is a card-based signaling system Toyota developed to coordinate the replenishment of parts on its assembly lines. It's very similar to our storyboard with a few key differences.

Sample Kanban Board

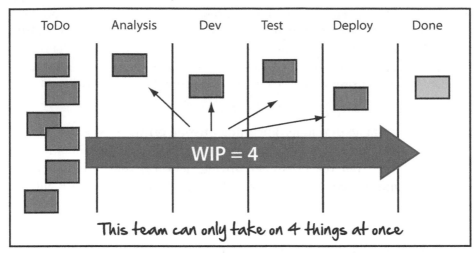

No fixed iteration length
No story/task limit size

* WIP: Work in progress

For one, in Kanban work is limited by a concept called *work in progress* (WIP). A team is only allowed to work on a finite number of things at once.

For example, if the team can handle only four things at once, then their WIP becomes four. Anything else that needs to be done gets thrown on the back burner and prioritized, and the team gets to it when they get to it.

The other thing that is different is that Kanban doesn't require iterations. You can simply take the next most important thing off the list and pull the work when your team is ready.

The goal of Kanban is flow. You want to flow things across the board as quickly as you can by working on only a few things at once. Here are some advantages to working this way:

- You don't have to get stressed about iterations.

  - If you are split between operations and project work, you no longer need to get stressed about being interrupted during an iteration (because of, say, production support issues) because there is no iteration. You simply pick up the next item when you are ready and don't have to reset iteration expectations as you go.

- You are not limited to taking on tasks that fit within a single iteration.

What If You Weren't Allowed to Track Bugs?

Imagine we were no longer allowed to track bugs on our projects. What would you have to do differently?

Well, for one, you'd have to squash bugs on the spot because you wouldn't be able track them.

Second, you would need a way of regression testing that was fast and cheap that ensured that when you did squash a bug, it was really dead and never worked its way back into your system.

Third, if you were producing a lot of bugs, you'd want to slow down to find out what was causing so much pain and take steps to fix the root cause.

This is the kind of attitude and behavior you want to foster on your team. It's not about debating which bug-tracking system you use. It's about thinking how you can write software so you don't need the bug tracker in the first place.

- – Although it's generally a good idea to break big things down, there may be times where something is just really big and you are going to need a couple of weeks to move it across the board. So be it.

- It's a nice way to manage expectations

  - – Most teams still do some form of estimation, or at least size their Kanban board tasks according to relative sizing (at least it's recommended if you want to set some kind of expectation around when you are going to get to something).

    But there is a certain simplicity to Kanban. It's kinda like, "Hey, dude. We're working hard here. We'll get to your stuff, but we can work on only four things at a time." No points. No need to explain estimates. Just simple life stuff. We can handle only so many things at once.

Now if all this sounds crazy, because we've just spent most of the book talking about how great iterations are, relax.

Agile iterations are powerful, and if you are doing project-based work with constraints around things such as time and money, in today's industrialized world of annual budgets, iterations are the way to go.

But agile is more than just iterations. Being agile means doing whatever works for you. So if working without iterations is better for you, go for it. Kanban is a great fit for operations/support teams that need to react quickly and don't have the luxury of fixed-length iterations.

My advice is to stick with fixed-length iterations. If you are just starting out and doing project-based work, you'll appreciate the discipline and rigor that comes with having to regularly deliver working software to your customer each and every week.

If you're doing operational type work, give Kanban a try. The principles are all the same. How you execute is slightly different.

To learn more about the latest and greatest on Kanban, check out this site:

http://finance.groups.yahoo.com/group/kanbandev/messages

You are now ready for your session with Master Sensei.

Master Sensei
and the
aspiring warrior

STUDENT: *Master, I am working on a data warehousing project, and we are charged with producing financial reports for senior executives. There is no way we can possibly produce something of value every week. The data warehouse alone will take at least a month to set up. How should I manage my iterations?*

MASTER: *The trick to delivering something of value is to focus on thin slices of functionality that go end-to-end through the application. Instead of building the data warehouse in its entirety, take a small subsection of one of your reports, and build only those pieces of the infrastructure that you need.*

STUDENT: *But what if even after doing that, we run into something that is so big we just can't fit it into an iteration?*

MASTER: *If it doesn't fit, it doesn't fit. Take as many iterations as you require to build the infrastructure and move on. Just remember that you want customer engagement. And telling them you are going to disappear for three months while you set things up makes them lose interest. It's much better for you and them if you can find a way to deliver something small and build on it each iteration thereafter.*

STUDENT: *Thank you, Master. I will think about this more.*

What's Next?

There you have it. Analysis, development, and testing, all rolled up into one to deliver something of value every week. Remember, there is no one way to do this stuff, and the artifacts and the way you work will need to change from project to project. So, don't be afraid to experiment and try different things.

With that behind us, we're now ready to see how agile teams communicate and coordinate all these simultaneously occurring activities during an iteration. Let's now take a look at the agile communication plan.

CHAPTER 10

Creating an Agile Communication Plan

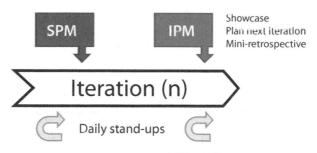

* SPM: Story planning meeting
* IPM: Iteration planning meeting

Other than suggesting that you co-locate your team and regularly put working software in front of your customer, agile doesn't give you much guidance in how to organize your iteration's work. It's up to you and your team to figure out how you want to organize, communicate, receive feedback, and pull things together.

In this chapter, you'll find out what critical components go into any agile communication plan and how to make one that works for you and your team.

By the end of the chapter, not only will you have a plan, but you'll have the beginnings of some rhythm and ritual for continuously producing something of value on your project.

10.1 Four Things to Do During Any Iteration

Two constants you'll find on any agile project are setting expectations and getting feedback.

Continuously setting expectations is necessary because things are always going to be changing. You will want to get in the habit of meeting regularly with your customer and reviewing the current state of your project.

And because the simple act of putting working software in the hands of your customer changes the requirements, you're going to want that strong feedback loop to make sure you're hitting the mark.

In that vein, there are four things you're going to want to do to get some rhythm and ritual going on each of your iterations:

- Make sure next iteration's work is ready (story-planning meeting).
- Get feedback on last iteration's stories (showcase).
- Plan the next iteration's work (iteration planning meeting).
- Continuously look for areas of improvement (mini-retrospective).

Let's start by looking at how we can make sure the next iteration's work is ready.

10.2 The Story-Planning Meeting

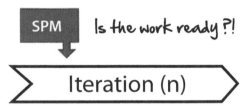

Have we done our homework?
Are next iteration's stories good to go?

This is our just-in-time analysis checkpoint meeting. During the SPM, we'll review test criteria for upcoming stories with the customer, review estimates with developers, and generally make sure we've done our homework on the next batch of iteration stories.

Sometimes you'll discover a story that's bigger than you thought. That's OK. Just break it down so it fits within a single iteration, update the plan, and move on. The good news is that this works both ways (we also find some stories are smaller than we had thought).

You won't find SPMs covered in any formal agile method. They are just one mechanism I and others have found useful for avoiding the waste that comes from starting an iteration with an unanalyzed story.

You're Going to Make Mistakes—Don't Sweat It

I was once working on a print story for this construction project, and I took the Spartan warrior route (delivering the bare-bones implementation). As soon as I demo'd it, I could tell the customer just didn't like it.

They were too polite to say anything, but I could feel it, and I knew it wasn't my best work.

At that point, I had to suck it up and ask them if I could try again. They said yes.

If I hadn't been delivering fiercely for seven weeks before this, they might have given me a different answer. But when your customer sees you busting your hump for them every week, they are going to be forgiving and cut you some slack for the occasional time you do screw up.

So, don't be afraid to try stuff. Trying and failing and taking initiative is part of the game.

But that's the beauty of agile. There's no one way to do this stuff. If you need something, create it or do it yourself (despite what any author or book says).

Something else you are going want to do every iteration is get some customer feedback.

10.3 The Showcase

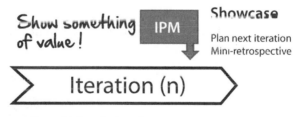

You made it! You delivered something of value. Do you know how many projects go for weeks, months, and sometimes years without delivering anything of value? A lot.

The *showcase* is your opportunity to show off to the world the great work you and the team have been doing and get some real honest-to-goodness feedback from your customer.

During a showcase, you and the entire team demo last iteration's stories. That means showing real live code deployed on a test server. It's not pretty pictures or best intentions. It's the stuff you could go to battle with and deploy today if you really had to. It's done.

Showcases are meant to be fun and are a great way to close out last iteration's work. Celebrate! Bring snacks or candy. Show off. Get feedback. Let your customer drive the demo and watch them use the software.

Let's now check out the one meeting agile methods like Scrum and XP do recommend you have—the iteration planning meeting (IPM).

10.4 Plan the Next Iteration

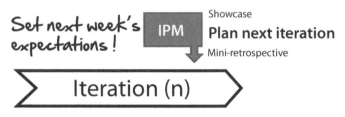

The IPM is where you get together with your customer and plan the next iteration's work. You review your team's velocity, you review upcoming stories, and then collectively figure out how much you and the team can commit to for next iteration's work.

IPMs are also a great time to do a mini-project health check.

Clear skies
- Smooth sailing
- Nothing slowing us down
- Things couldn't be better

Few clouds, chance of rain
- We're delivering
- Experiencing some turbulence
- But nothing we can't handle

Big storm
- Houston, we have a problem
- Major challenges ahead
- We need help!

Here you can give a quick weather forecast about how the project is doing. If there is something you need or there is a particularly hairy problem you'd like to discuss, this is your opportunity to raise the issue, present some options, and make some recommendations on how you'd like to proceed.

When it comes to talking about dates, use your burn-down chart. It's brutally honest, and in a very unemotional way, it will tell you and your customer how realistic your dates are looking.

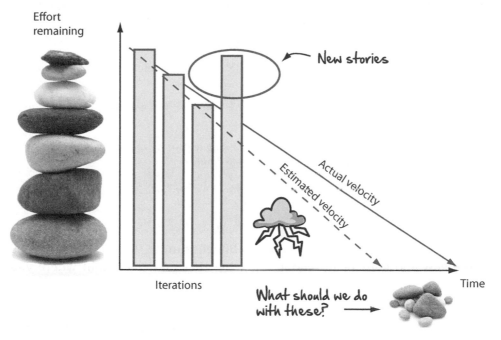

This is the visibility part of agile. We want to be as transparent as possible with our customers and stakeholders. Bad news early is the agile way.

The final thing we want to do before leaving any iteration is ask ourselves whether there's anything we could be doing better.

10.5 How to Host a Mini-Retrospective

Agile principle

At regular intervals, the team reflects on how to become more effective and then tunes and adjusts its behavior accordingly.

Retrospectives can be big, fancy, all-day affairs that are held at the end of a major release or near the end of a project. That's not what I am talking about here.

How to Give Constructive Feedback

There's two ways to give feedback. You can serve it up straight and cold:

- "Suzy, I noticed you did some great work on the print module last iteration, *but* your unit tests were really lacking."

Or you can add a drop of honey and sweeten it up a bit:

- "Suzy, awesome work on the print module. Apply that same level of detail to your unit tests, and you are soon going to be world-class."

See the difference? By avoiding the use of the word *but*, you can totally change the tone and delivery of the message.

I'm not saying you need to coat everything in sugar. But by changing the message sometimes, you can go a long way to changing behavior.

To get the full scope on how to communicate effectively, read the Dale Carnegie classic *How to Win Friends and Influence People [Car90]*.

These retrospectives are quick, ten- to fifteen-minute, focused discussions where you and your team regularly get together and talk about where you are kicking butt and where you need to improve.

The first rule of thumb for hosting a good retrospective is to make sure everyone feels safe. If you think you have an issue with safety, pull out the retrospective prime directive and remind people what it's all about.

The retrospective prime directive

Regardless of what we discover, we understand and truly believe that everyone did the best job they could, given what they knew at the time, their skills and abilities, the resources available, and the situation at hand.

In other words it's not a witch hunt.

Then you can warm people up by asking the first retrospective question.

1. What we are doing really well?

"Jimmy, good job on those unit tests, mate."

"Suzy. That was so awesome how you created that style guide and refactored the style sheets so we can easily maintain a constant look and feel across our application."

Calling out good behavior and giving props to people who deserve to be recognized can put wind in people's sails and encourage more of the kind of behavior we like seeing on our projects.

The other side of the equation is talking about where we can improve.

2. Where do we need to be better?

"Team, a lot of bugs got through that last batch of stories. Let's slow down, tighten things up, and make sure we are doing enough unit testing."

"We're seeing a lot of duplication going on in the code base. Remember to take the time and refactor the code as you go."

"I completely blew that print story. I am sorry. Let me have another whack at it this iteration, and I promise you the next version will be much better."

Whatever the issue, holding a retrospective, and sharing ideas with teammates is a great way to refocus and energize the team on those areas they need to shore up. Then you can create a theme for the next couple iterations and highlight and track those areas you want to improve.

For the definitive guide to holding retrospectives, check out *Agile Retrospectives: Making Good Teams Great [DL06]*.

Good stuff. Let's wrap by going over a great way to quickly align everyone at the start of the day—the daily stand-up.

10.6 How Not to Host a Daily Stand-Up

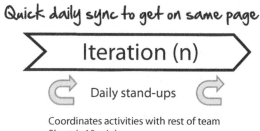

The daily stand-up is about sharing important information with your team quickly. It's the meeting to end all meetings. It's five to ten minutes long, no chairs are required (to remind people to keep it brief), and you basically give an update on what you're working on and share anything you think the rest of the team needs to know.

Now, most agile textbooks will tell you that when doing a daily stand-up you should stand in a circle and have everyone on the team tell everyone the following:

- What they did yesterday
- What they're doing today
- Whether there is anything slowing them down

Good information. It's just not very inspiring or behavior changing.

Instead, try getting together with your team at the beginning of each day and instead tell them the following:

- What you did to change the world yesterday
- How you are going to crush it today
- How you are going to blast through any obstacles unfortunate enough to be standing in your way

Answering these types of questions completely changes the dynamic of the stand-up. Instead of just standing there and giving an update, you are now laying it all on the line and declaring your intent to the universe.

When you do this, one of two things is going to happen. Either you are going to follow through and deliver or you're not. It's completely up to you.

But I can tell you this: if you show up every day and publicly declare to your peers what you are personally committed to doing that day, it dramatically increases the chances of you getting it done.

10.7 Do Whatever Works for You

Now in case you are wondering whether these all need to be separate meetings or whether you can roll them all up into one...it's completely up to you.

To keep the number of meetings down to a minimum, some teams like to combine the showcase, next iteration planning, and retro all into one and do it in an hour (that's my preference, and that's what I've presented here under one IPM).

Others prefer separating the planning from the showcases and doing the retro as a fun activity near the end of the week.

And some teams have such good contact with their customers that they don't need dedicated story-planning meetings (SPMs). They just talk every day and have a design session whenever they need it.

Remember, there is no one way to do this stuff. If something isn't adding value, drop it. Try different things out and see what works for you.

Just make sure that at some point during your iteration you get in front of your customer, show them some working software, set expectations, and look for ways to improve.

Uh-oh. It's looks like Master Sensei wants to see whether you're picking any of this stuff up. Better get on over to the dojo and see whether any of this stuff makes sense. Good luck!

Master Sensei and the aspiring warrior

Welcome back, Student. I have prepared for you three lessons to test your mettle on several real-life iteration mechanic scenarios. Please read each carefully before answering.

Scenario #1: The Incomplete Story

MASTER: *One day, during an IPM, it became apparent that a story was only half complete. Wanting to show progress, the young project manager wanted to count half of the story's points toward this iteration's team velocity and then count the other half when the story was completed next iteration. Is this a good idea?*

STUDENT: *Well, if the story is truly half done, I see no harm in accurately reflecting the state of the story by counting half the story's points toward this iteration's velocity and carrying over the other half to the next iteration.*

MASTER: *Is that so? Answer me this. Can a farmer transport his rice on a wagon with one wheel? Can a man eat with but one chopstick? Can a customer go into production with half a feature?*

STUDENT: *No, Sensei?*

MASTER: *To the agile warrior there is no 1/2 , 3/4 done, or 4/5 done for a user story. The story is complete, or it is not. For that reason, the warrior only counts fully tested and completed stories toward his iteration's velocity. Any uncompleted stories are carried over.*

Scenario #2: Daily Stand-Ups Are Not Adding Value

MASTER: *Once there was a team struggling to get members to attend their daily stand-ups. Team members thought the meetings weren't adding much value and that they could be better off working and speaking to each other when necessary. What should the team do?*

STUDENT: *The leader of the team should remind everyone of the importance of keeping everyone on the same page and the important role the daily stand-up plays in achieving that.*

MASTER: *Yes. The team could review the goals of the daily stand-up and why it was created in the first place. But what if, despite that, the team still feels the meetings are unnecessary?*

STUDENT: *I'm not following you, Sensei. How could bringing everyone together quickly every day, and getting everyone up to speed on the project, ever be considered a waste of time?*

MASTER: *Despite all the benefits that come from a good daily stand-up, it is not the only way. If a team is co-located, is small, and works closely with one another and their customer continuously throughout the day, a daily stand-up may not always be required.*

STUDENT: *Are you saying some teams don't need daily stand-ups?*

MASTER: *I am saying teams should keep those practices that add value. They should modify or drop those that do not.*

Scenario #3: The Iteration Where Nothing of Value Was Produced

MASTER: *There was once a team that went a full iteration without being able to deliver anything of value. The failure was entirely in their own making. They failed to plan, they started late, and they were generally lazy. Knowing this was going to be a tough message to deliver, they canceled the showcase with their customer. Was this wise?*

STUDENT: *Although part of me feels like the team should face the music for not delivering anything of value, I suppose if they have nothing to show, canceling the showcase would be acceptable. However, I would rather they be honest as to why.*

MASTER: *Ah...you are becoming wise, student. Not delivering anything of value does happen from time to time, but usually not by design or because of lack of effort. How can the team correct this laziness in behavior?*

STUDENT: Are you suggesting they keep the showcase, Master? And face their customers while having nothing of value to show?

MASTER: Hai! Sometimes feeling the sting of shame is the best teacher. Facing your customers and having nothing to show can be a humbling experience. Once experienced, it is not something teams will ever want to do again.

STUDENT: Thank you, Master. I will contemplate this more.

Do not seek to avoid unpleasant situations on your project. They are sometimes your best teacher. Admit your mistakes, share what you have learned with others, and move on.

What's Next?

With a communication plan in hand and a good understanding of how iterative development works, you're in a good place to see how the best agile teams turn it up a notch when it comes to executing fiercely.

Next up, you are going to learn the secrets of the visual work space and how to harness it to keep you and your team energized and focused.

CHAPTER 11

Setting Up a Visual Workspace

Flight status boards are great. In one quick glance you can see what's coming, what's going, and what's been canceled altogether.

Why not do the same for your project?

By learning how to create a visual workspace, you and the team will never be at a loss for what to do next or where you can add the greatest value. Not only will this enable you to work with greater clarity and focus, the increased transparency will also help you set expectations with the powers that be.

Speaking of which, here they come now.

11.1 Uh-oh...Here Come the Heavies!

There's been a big shake-up at corporate. Budgets have been cut. Timelines have been slashed. And now everything needs to be done better, faster, and cheaper.

As a result, you've been asked to do more with less. Management would like you to deliver the same amount of functionality, with half the team, one month ahead of schedule. Or else.

It's all coming down hard and fast, and tomorrow they want to set up a meeting with you to confirm you are on board with the new plan.

Gulp! What do you do? What they are asking for is completely unreasonable. You know it. The team knows. It seems they are the only ones who don't.

What could you do to show that while you would love nothing more than to be able to deliver the same amount of functionality with half the resources, it ain't gonna happen.

Bringing the Executives Up to Speed

Instead of setting up a formal meeting and pleading your case in PowerPoint, you invite the executives down to your work area to see firsthand the state of the project.

You begin by taking them through the inception deck for your project, which you conveniently have posted on the wall.

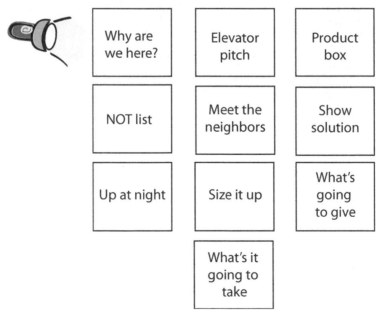

The inception deck, you explain, is a tool you and the team use to make sure you never lose sight of the goal of the project. By making it visible, you always know who the customer is, what they're after, and, most important, why we decided to spend money on this project in the first place.

Impressed, the executives lean closer and ask you where you are in the project. To answer that, you then direct their attention to your *release wall*.

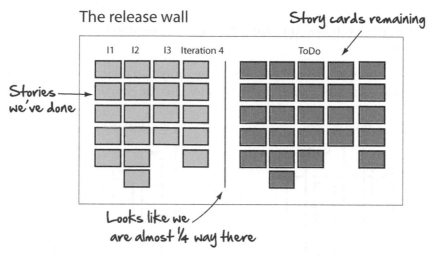

The release wall is where you and the team keep track of what's been done and what's remaining. The left side of the wall shows those features that have been fully analyzed, developed, tested, and vetted by the customer (they are ready to be shipped). And the right side shows those stories still needing to be developed.

As far as what the team is working on this iteration, you draw management's attention over to this iteration's storyboard.

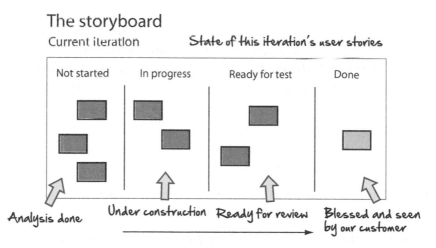

The storyboard tracks the state of this iteration's features (or what we call *user stories*). Features yet to be developed live on the left, while those that have been built and blessed by the customer live on the right. As a story gets more developed, it moves across the board from left to right. Only when it is fully developed, tested, and vetted by the customer does it get moved into the Done column.

Looking at their watches, they then cut to the chase and ask when *you* expect to be done.

To answer that, you bring them over to the only two charts on your wall you haven't shown them yet—your team velocity and the project burn-down chart.

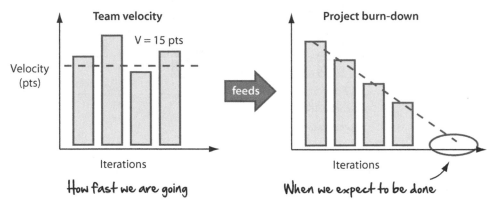

You explain that the team velocity is the closest thing you and the team have for measuring the team's level of productivity. By measuring how much the team gets done each week and using that as the basis of planning going forward, the team can accurately predict when they expect to be done. This is shown on the project burn-down chart.

The project burn-down (see above in Section 8.5, *The Burn-Down Chart*, on page 128) takes the team velocity and extrapolates the speed at which the team is "burning" through the customer's wish list. The project is done when the team delivers everything on the list or the project runs out of money (whichever comes first).

With the stage set, you now calmly point out what should already be obvious to everyone in the room. Halving the development team would effectively cut the team's productivity in half.

Impressed with your command of the situation, the executives thank you for your time and move onto their next project meeting.

A few weeks later you get an email explaining that because of the company's heading in a new strategic direction, your project is going to be canceled (life is like that sometimes).

The good news, however, is that they were so impressed with how you managed your project, they want you to play a lead role in the new initiative!

This is just one contrived example of how a visual workspace can help you set expectations with stakeholders and make the reality of a situation self-evident. But where it really shines is in helping you and your team execute and focus.

Let's now go over some ideas for creating your own visual workspace.

11.2 How to Create a Visual Workspace

Creating a good visual workspace is pretty straightforward. For teams new to agile, I usually recommend starting with the following:

- A story wall
- A release wall
- A velocity and burn-down graph
- An inception deck, if they have the room

The inception deck is good because it reminds the team why they are there and what it's really all about (which can be easy to lose sight of when your head is buried in your project).

The story wall is great because any morning anyone can walk in and know exactly what needs to be done next.

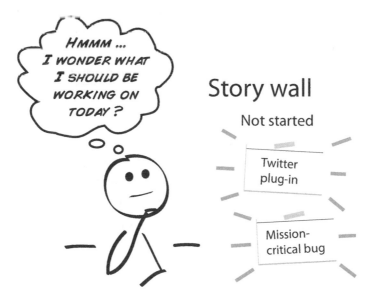

The story wall will also show you any bottlenecks you have in the system and where you'll want to direct resources.

The storyboard
Current iteration

GUESS I BETTER
SHIFT GEARS
AND TEST!!!

Not started   In progress   Ready for test   Done

The agile developer

Resources needed here!

The release wall is a thing of beauty, because anyone can walk into your room and see the state of your project at a glance. This is what's done. This is what's remaining. No fancy math or Excel spreadsheets required.

And as we talked about extensively in agile planning, nothing sets expectations better than a good burn-down chart. Keep one of these babies on your wall, and you'll always know how realistic your dates are looking and how you are trending.

And of course this is just the beginning. If you have other pictures, mock-ups, or diagrams that help you and your team execute, stick 'em up there and make it visible for all to see.

Here are some other ideas for creating your visual workspace.

11.3 Show Your Intent

Working agreements are about putting a stake in the ground as a team and saying, "This is how we as a team like to work." It's a way of setting expectations with everyone on the team about how your team is going to work and what's going to be expected of people if they join you on this ride.

Shared values are the same, only more touchy-feely. If the team has been burned in the past because they were forced to compromise on quality and no longer want to be known as that team that cuts corners and writes crappy software, they can post their shared values and make that known.

Working agreements	Shared values
* Core hours 9 a.m.-4 p.m.	* We don't cut corners
* Daily stand-ups 10 a.m. sharp	* No broken windows
* Done includes testing	* It's OK to disagree
* Respect the build	* We can handle the truth
* When someone asks you for help say "yes"	* Don't assume—ask
	* When in doubt—write a test
* Weekly demo Tues 11am	* Crave feedback
* Customer available 1-3 p.m.	* Check your ego at the door

The other thing you want to be sure you share on your project is language.

11.4 Create and Share a Common Domain Language

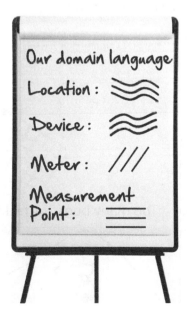

When the words used in your software don't match those used by business, you can get into all sorts of trouble.

- The wrong abstractions get built into the software (business will think *location* means one thing, while developers will interpret it to mean something else).

- The software becomes harder to change (because the words that appear on the screen don't match those used to store it in the database).

- You end up with more bugs and higher maintenance costs (because the team has to work extra hard when making changes to the software).

To avoid this dysfunction, create a common language that you and the business share and use it relentlessly in your user stories, models, pictures, and code.

For example, if there are some key words that you and your customer use when you talk about the system, write them down, come up with clear definitions about what these words mean, and then make sure you match those definitions on the software (that is, screens, code, and database columns). Doing this will not only minimize the bugs and rework but also make it way easier to talk to your customer because your code will always be in lockstep with how they talk about their business.

We don't have the time or space to do this topic justice. But there is an excellent book on the subject by Eric Evans: *Domain-Driven Design: Tackling Complexity in the Heart of Software. [Eva03]*. It's well worth the read.

Finally, watch your bugs.

11.5 Watch Those Bugs

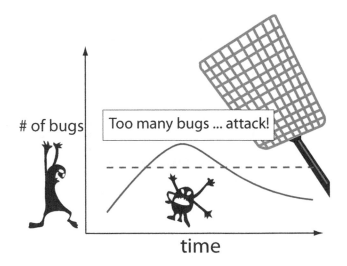

To make sure you and your team aren't overwhelmed by a surprise bug attack just before you roll into production, track and keep your bug count down from day one of your project.

If it helps, dedicate 10 percent of every iteration to bug squashing and paying down technical debt. Just squash those buggers on the spot, and don't let that bug count get away from you.

Master Sensei and the aspiring warrior

STUDENT: *Master, what if my workplace does not allow me to create a visual workspace? What should I do?*

MASTER: *It is true that some office work environments resist project teams putting their work artifacts up on the wall. When faced with this resistance, accept that it is there and decide how to proceed.*

STUDENT: *Yes, Master. But should I fight for the visual workspace? Or just accept that I can't have one?*

MASTER: *That is up to you. You can compromise. You can acquiesce. Or you can confront. There is a time and place for each. Search your heart, seek allies, and decide whether this battle is worth the effort.*

STUDENT: *If this is truly an important practice, what can one do to compromise?*

MASTER: *When faced with situations such as these, some warriors have found creating fold-away storyboards useful for keeping the workplace clean, while enabling the team to communicate openly during the day. Others have used online tools and virtual storyboards for sharing important information, as well as keeping the team in sync.*

STUDENT: *So, my visual workspace doesn't always have to be physical?*

MASTER: *No. Physical is best but sometimes not always possible.*

STUDENT: *What if I choose to confront? What should I do then?*

MASTER:

You can start by simply creating a visual workspace, use it daily for your project, and hope that, through dialogue and education, the benefits become self-evident.

STUDENT: *And if they do not?*

MASTER: *Then the root cause is usually one based on emotion. There may be forces diametrically opposed to what you are trying to achieve. Try empathizing and understanding the spirit behind those forces arrayed against you. Perhaps through dialogue, you will be able to find a solution that works for both parties. Time and patience may be your best allies here.*

What's Next?

Your journey is almost complete. You've got everyone on the bus (Chapter 3, *How to Get Everyone on the Bus*, on page 35), you've got the plan (Chapter 8, *Agile Planning: Dealing with Reality*, on page 113), and you know what it takes to execute.

The next part of the book, "Agile Software Engineering," focuses on the core agile software engineering practices you and your team are going to need to make all this agile stuff happen.

It's a must-read if you cut code, but it is also recommended if you ever plan on leading an agile project. None of this agile stuff works unless it's backed by some really solid technical practices, and although each of the next four chapters could be a book in themselves, the chapters here will give you enough of a taste to understand how the practices work and why they are important for your team's overall agility.

We'll start by taking a look at one of the greatest time-savers of any software project—automated unit testing.

Part V

Creating Agile Software

CHAPTER 12

Unit Testing: Knowing It Works

For all the time spent on planning and managing expectations, agile processes don't work unless they're backed by a solid set of software engineering practices. Although some practices—such as XP's pair programming—have been controversial, others such as automated unit testing have become widely accepted.

In the final four chapters of the book, we're going to learn about what I like to refer to as the no-brainers of agile software engineering:

- Unit testing
- Refactoring
- Test-driven development (TDD)
- Continuous integration

Each one of these chapters could easily be a book in itself, but by introducing the concepts to you here, you'll at least have a good understanding of what they are and know enough of the mechanics to get you and your team going.

All examples are in Microsoft .NET C# (though the concepts can be applied to all languages in general). And don't worry if you are the nontechnical type.

This is good stuff for you to be aware of, and I will highlight the important stuff as we go.

Let's start with the one practice that underpins most of what we do when it comes to agile software engineering: rigorous and extensive unit testing.

12.1 Welcome to Vegas, Baby!

You lucky dog! You've just joined a team of software developers building a new Black Jack simulator! Your first task is design a deck of cards.

Here's your first cut of the code in C# for a full deck of cards:

```
tdd/src/Deck.cs
public class Deck
{
    private readonly IList<Card> cards = new List<Card>();

    public Deck()
    {
        cards.Add(Card.TWO_OF_CLUBS);
        cards.Add(Card.THREE_OF_CLUBS);
        // .. remaining clubs

        cards.Add(Card.TWO_OF_DIAMONDS);
        cards.Add(Card.THREE_OF_DIAMONDS);
        // ... remaining diamonds

        cards.Add(Card.TWO_OF_SPADES);
        cards.Add(Card.THREE_OF_SPADES);
        // ... remaining spades

        cards.Add(Card.TWO_OF_HEARTS);
        cards.Add(Card.THREE_OF_HEARTS);
        // ... remaining hearts

        // joker
        cards.Add(Card.JOKER);
    }
}
```

You make it through peer review, everything looks good, and just before you're set to roll into production, QA finds a bug. There is no joker card in a Black Jack deck! You fix the bug, give QA a new build, and release into production.

Then a couple weeks later you get a nasty email from the QA manager informing you that there was a major bug in production last night. Tens of thousands of dollars needed to be reimbursed because someone put a joker in the Card class!

> ## Write a Failing Unit Test Before Fixing the Bug
>
> When you discover a bug in your software, it's tempting to jump right in there and fix it. Don't. Instead, first capture the bug in the form of a failing unit test, and then fix it. Doing this will ensure the following:
>
> - Prove you understand the nature of the bug
> - Give you confidence you've fixed it
> - Ensure that the bug can never burrow its way back into your program again

"What?" you say. "Impossible. I fixed that bug a couple weeks ago." Digging deeper, you discover that a summer student you were mentoring took you a little too literally when you asked her to make sure your deck of cards class behaved just like a physical deck of cards you gave her to test against.

It seems she inadvertently added the joker back into the deck, thinking she had found a bug.

Ashamed and embarrassed, the summer student apologizes to you and the rest of the team. Behind closed doors, she asks you what she can do to make sure something like this never happens again.

What do you tell her? What could she (or you) have done to make sure that the joker bug had zero chance of ever reentering the code base once it had been fixed?

In this light, let's now take a look at the humble unit test.

12.2 Enter the Unit Test

Unit tests are small, method-level tests developers write every time they make a change to the software to prove the changes they made work as expected.

For example, say we wanted to verify our deck of cards had fifty-two cards in it (and not fifty-three). We could write a unit test that would look something like this:

tdd/test/DeckTest.cs
```
[TestFixture]
public class DeckTest
{
    [Test]
    public void Verify_deck_contains_52_cards()
    {
        var deck = new Deck();
        Assert.AreEqual(52, deck.Count());
    }
}
```

Just to be clear, the previous code isn't the actual code we run as part of our Black Jack simulator in production. This is test code that verifies our real code works as expected.

Whenever we have a doubt about how our code is going to behave or we want to verify it's doing what we expect, we write a unit test (in this case one that verifies our deck has fifty-two cards).

Unit tests are invaluable because once we automate and make them easy to run, we can run them every time we make a change to our software and know instantly whether we broke something (more on this in Chapter 15, *Continuous Integration: Making It Production-Ready*, on page 217).

Typically agile projects will have hundreds if not thousands of unit tests. They will slice right through the entire application testing everything from our application's business logic down to whether we can store our customer's information in the database.

The benefits of writing lots of these against your code base are many:

- They give you instant feedback.

  – When you make changes to your code and a unit test breaks, you know about that instantly (not three weeks later after you've rolled into production).

- They dramatically lower the cost of regression testing.

  – Instead of having to manually retest everything every time we pump out a new release, we save ourselves a ton of time by automating the easy stuff so we have more time to test the complicated stuff.

- They greatly reduce debugging time.

  – When a unit test fails, you know exactly where the problem is. No more firing up the debugger and stepping through thousands of lines of code, searching for the offending piece of code. Unit tests cut through the fog like a laser and show exactly where the problem is.

- They let you deploy with confidence.

  – It just feels good rolling into production knowing you have a suite of automated tests backing you up. They're not foolproof, but they free you up to test the other more interesting/complicated parts of your system.

Test Everything That Could Possibly Break

Extreme Programming (XP) has a mantra called "test everything that could possibly break." It is a reminder to developers that if there is something they think stands a reasonable chance of breaking the system, then they should write an automated test against it.

We can never test everything, but the practice does capture the spirit of how agile wants teams to think about testing. Test as much as you think you need to make sure your software is working, and use your judgment to figure out where you can get the most testing bang for your buck.

In Chapter 14, *Test-Driven Development*, on page 207, we'll see how test-driving development can help you figure out where to maximize your testing dollars, as well as strike the right balance between trying to test everything vs. testing just enough.

Think of unit tests as the armor you don before riding into battle. They become a form of executable spec that lives forever in your code, protecting you from missiles, real and imaginary dragons, and, most importantly, ourselves.

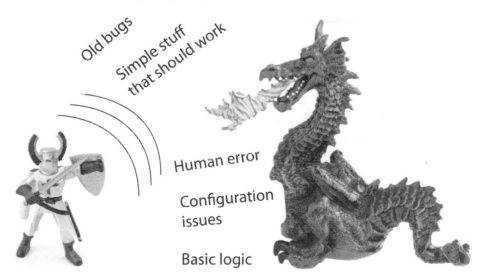

Warning: you will also periodically run into cases where writing an automated test is tough. For example, writing a test to verify we could shuffle our deck of cards is hard (as the answer is random and would change every time). Also, testing concurrency and multithreaded applications can be challenging, to say the least.

When you run into cases like these, don't despair. They are the exception rather than the norm. In the overwhelming number of cases, you are going to be able to instantiate an object and make assertions on the methods you call. This is even more possible with all the unit testing mocking frameworks available today.

In those rare cases where you can't test something readily, it may be an issue with your design (see Chapter 14, *Test-Driven Development*, on page 207). Or maybe you've inherited some legacy code that is just really hard to test.

If this is the case, so be it. Accept that you won't be able to test everything. Make sure you cover it with some really good manual and exploratory testing, and move on.

Just don't give up! Always try to automate that chunk of code, because having that little extra bit of armor can really save your bacon when that emergency bug fix request comes in and you have to get a release out fast.

You can also read Michael Feathers' *Working Effectively with Legacy Code [Fea04]*, which has lots of invaluable suggestions for how to take tough to work with legacy code and make it more open to change.

Let's get you thinking like a tester. What unit tests do you think we could write against our deck of cards class given the following requirements? How could we prevent that nasty joker bug from ever appearing again?

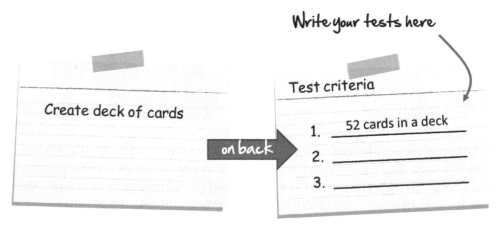

If your tests look something like these, you are on the right track. We want to test everything that could possibly break, so if you suspect that something could go wrong, put yourself at ease and write a test.

```
tdd/test/DeckTest.cs
[TestFixture]
public class DeckTest2
{
    [Test]
    public void Verify_deck_contains_52_cards()
    {
        var deck = new Deck();
        Assert.AreEqual(52, deck.Count());
    }

    [Test]
    public void Verify_deck_contains_thirteen_cards_for_each_suit()
    {
        var Deck = new Deck();
        Assert.AreEqual(13, Deck.NumberOfHearts());
        Assert.AreEqual(13, Deck.NumberOfClubs());
        Assert.AreEqual(13, Deck.NumberOfDiamonds());
        Assert.AreEqual(13, Deck.NumberOfSpades());
    }

    [Test]
    public void Verify_deck_contains_no_joker()
    {
        var Deck = new Deck();
        Assert.IsFalse(Deck.Contains(Card.JOKER));
    }

    [Test]
    public void Check_every_card_in_the_deck()
    {
        var Deck = new Deck();

        Assert.IsTrue(Deck.Contains(Card.TWO_OF_CLUBS));
        Assert.IsTrue(Deck.Contains(Card.TWO_OF_DIAMONDS));
        Assert.IsTrue(Deck.Contains(Card.TWO_OF_HEARTS));
        Assert.IsTrue(Deck.Contains(Card.TWO_OF_SPADES));

        Assert.IsTrue(Deck.Contains(Card.THREE_OF_CLUBS));
        Assert.IsTrue(Deck.Contains(Card.THREE_OF_DIAMONDS));
        Assert.IsTrue(Deck.Contains(Card.THREE_OF_HEARTS));
        Assert.IsTrue(Deck.Contains(Card.THREE_OF_SPADES));

        // the others
    }
}
```

For you nontechies, the previous code contains unit tests that do the following:

- Check each deck has thirteen cards for each suit

- Ensure our deck does not contain any jokers (this is the bug that slipped through earlier)

- Check every card in the deck (all fifty-two of them)

Where Can I Learn More?

We've only scratched the surface of unit testing, and a lot more can be said on the subject. Fortunately, unit testing is becoming so common on software projects that most modern languages have unit testing frameworks (freely available for download) and tutorials showing you how to get started.

A good place to start for any developer looking to understand the spirit of the practice is Kent Beck's classic introductory paper.[1]

You can also check out *Pragmatic Unit Testing in C# with NUnit [TH04]* and *Pragmatic Unit Testing in Java with JUnit [TH03]*.

Master Sensei
and the
aspiring warrior

STUDENT: Master, how does unit testing not slow teams down? I mean, you're writing double the amount of code, aren't you?

MASTER: If programming were merely typing, that would be true. The unit tests are there to confirm that as we make changes to our software, the universe still unfolds as expected. This saves us time by not having to manually regression test the entire system every time we make a change.

QUESTION: Yes, Master. But won't writing unit tests make the code brittle? How do I ensure that my unit tests won't break every time I make a change to my code?

---

1.   http://junit.sourceforge.net/doc/testinfected/testing.htm

ANSWER: *Although it is certainly possible to write brittle tests that rely on hard-coded data, are tightly coupled, and are poorly designed, as you become accustomed to letting the tests drive your design (Chapter 14, Test-Driven Development, on page 207), you will find your tests do tend not to break and in fact improve your overall design. Most modern integrated development environments (IDEs) also make handling changes to your code and tests easy. You can rename a method throughout your entire code base by simply pressing a few keys. This helps keep your tests and production moving as one.*

QUESTION: *Is 100 percent unit test coverage something I and my team should shoot for?*

ANSWER: *No. The point of unit testing isn't coverage—it's giving yourself and your team enough confidence that your software is sound and ready for production.*

QUESTION: *So, then, how much unit test coverage should I and my team have?*

ANSWER: *That is for you and your team to decide. Some frameworks and languages make achieving good test coverage easy. Others make achieving good coverage hard. If you are just starting out, do not be overly concerned with coverage. Just write as many of the best tests that you can.*

What's Next?

Good job. You now know of one of the core underpinnings upon which all our other agile software engineering practices rest. Without sound automated unit tests, it all falls apart.

Next we are going to look at how to build on our unit tests and do something so critical that were we to somehow skip this practice, our product would become just another overpriced, unmaintainable blob of code resistant to all forms of change.

Let's now look at the important practice of refactoring.

CHAPTER 13

Refactoring: Paying Down Your Technical Debt

Just like a house with a mortgage, software has debt that continuously needs to be paid down too.

In this chapter, we are going to look at the practice of refactoring and see how by regularly paying down the technical debt we can keep our software nimble and flexible and our house a joy to work and live in.

By the end of the chapter, you'll see how refactoring will lower your maintenance costs, give you a common vocabulary for making improvements to the code, and enable you to add new functionality at full speed.

Let's now enter the world of refactoring and see what it takes to turn on a dime.

13.1 Turn on a Dime

It seems the competition has just released a "kid-friendly" version of your company's online Black Jack product—and it's selling like hot cakes.

To respond to this new competitive threat, you and the team start work immediately, and for a while everything is going all right. But then something strange starts to happen. What initially looked like a slam dunk is now starting to look really hard.

For one, a lot of code has been copied and pasted throughout the code base. This is making adding new functionality hard because every time you make a change in one place, you need to make the same change in a dozen others.

On top of that, the code you and the team wrote in haste to hit the last deadline has now come back to haunt you. It's really a mess and hard to work with. To make matters worse, the programmer who originally wrote it is now long gone.

Here's just one sample from the offending code:

Refactoring/src/BlackJack.cs
```
public bool DealerWins(Hand hand1)
{
    var h1 = hand1; int sum1 =0;
    foreach (var c in h1)
    {
        sum1 += Value(c.Value, h1);
    }
    var h2 = DealerManager.Hand; int sum2 =0;
    foreach (var c in h2)
    {
        sum2 += Value(c.Value, h2);
    }

    if (sum2>=sum1)
    {
        return true;
    }
    else
        return false;

    return false;
}
```

Don't worry if you can't make sense of this code (I can't either). Yet this is the code you need to change. This is the code you need to maintain. This is the code you (ack!) pushed into production.

Working and making changes to this code base is going to take longer and cost more than you originally thought.

It quickly becomes apparent that to do this right, you are going to need at least two weeks just to clean up the existing code base before you can even start adding the new functionality. Unfortunately, that's two weeks of time your boss says you don't have.

What went wrong? How could something that was nice, simple, and easy to work with morph into something so big, ugly, and hard to work with?

We are now ready to take a look at a concept called *technical debt*.

13.2 Technical Debt

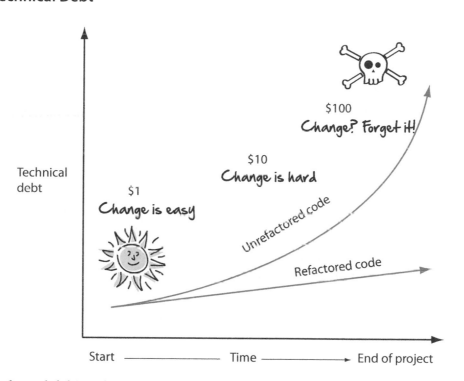

Technical debt is the continuous accumulation of shortcuts, hacks, duplication, and other sins we regularly commit against our code base in the name of speed and schedule.

You are always going to have some debt in your code (having none would mean you aren't trying innovative or different things), but you'll know you've accumulated too much when what used to be fun, easy, and simple is now painful, hard, and complex.

Technical debt can take many forms (spaghetti code, excessive complexity, duplication, and general sloppiness), but what makes it really dangerous is how it just kind of sneaks up on you. Each transgression initially made against the code base can seem small or insignificant. But like all forms of debt, it's the cumulative effect that adds up over time that hurts.

13.3 Make Payments Through Refactoring

Refactoring is the practice of continuously making small, incremental design improvements to your software without changing the overall external behavior.

When we refactor our code, we aren't adding new functionality or even fixing bugs. Instead, we are improving the understandability of our code by making it easier to comprehend and more amenable to change.

We call one of these changes a *refactoring*.

For example, whenever you rename a poorly named method or variable in an effort to make it easier to read and understand, you're refactoring.

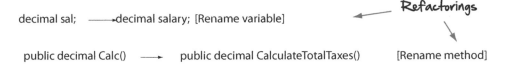

```
decimal sal;  ──────▶decimal salary; [Rename variable]          ◀── Refactorings

public decimal Calc()  ──────▶  public decimal CalculateTotalTaxes()          [Rename method]
```

At first glance, refactorings like these may seem small and insignificant. But when applied continuously and aggressively against a code base, they can have a profound impact on the quality and maintainability of the code.

For example, take look at these code snippets, and ask yourself which takes more effort to read and understand:

```
if (Date.Before(SUMMER_START) || Date.After(SUMMER_END))
    charge = quantity * _winterRate + _winterServiceCharge;
else
    charge = quantity * _summerRate;
```

OR ...

Refactoring: [Extract method]

```
if (NotSummer(date))
    charge = WinterCharge(quantity);
else
    charge = SummerCharge(quantity);
```

Technical Debt Is More Than Just Code

While most of our technical debt is code centric, you can also have it in data and build and configuration files.

What we need is a way of systematically paying down our technical debt as we go. We need a way of incrementally improving and maintaining our software's integrity and design that lets us meet the goals of today and be in a good position to handle the yet unknown challenges coming tomorrow.

In agile, we call this *refactoring*.

I was once part of a large-scale rewrite for a back-end system where a city name was spelled two different ways. The cost of this seemingly small difference was huge. Instead of not caring how the city was spelled, they had to write and carry this extra code and complexity for as long as that system remained in production, which for mainframe systems can be a very long time.

You don't have to be a developer or know C# to see that the second example is way easier to read and understand than the first. Writing code is a lot like writing good prose. You want it to be clear, easy to understand, and not take a lot of effort to figure out what's going on.

Refactoring is the secret sauce that object-oriented programmers use to do this. By choosing well-named methods and variables and hiding unnecessary detail from the reader, they are able to communicate their intent very clearly, making the code easy to understand and easy to change.

Agile principle

Continuous attention to technical excellence and good design enhances agility.

At its heart, that is what refactoring is really all about: reminding ourselves that software is written and maintained by folks like you and me. And if we can't make our software easy to change and a joy to work with, it's not going to be a lot of fun whenever we need to make changes or add new functionality.

Refactor Hard—Continuously

When you refactor aggressively, you don't slow down near the end of a project —you speed up. That's because when you've kept your design up over time, you've done most of the heavy lifting. New features build on older, well-designed ones. You can then leverage your hard work and reap the rewards from keeping a house in order.

Refactoring aggressively means not saving up all your refactorings until the end of an iteration. This is stuff you want to be doing continuously throughout the day.

When it's done right, refactoring is almost invisible. The steps are so small and the improvements so minute, it's almost impossible to tell the difference between when someone is refactoring the code and adding new functionality.

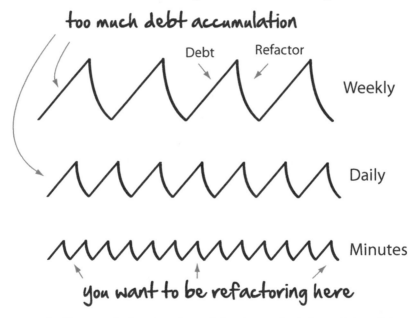

That's enough theory. Let's give the ol' brain a stretch and try this out for ourselves:

What improvements could we make to the kid-friendly version of our Black Jack game we saw at the beginning of the chapter?

```
public bool DealerWins(Hand hand1)
{
    var h1 = hand1; int sum1 =0;
    foreach (var c in h1)
    {
        sum1 += Value(c.Value, h1);
    }
    var h2 = DealerManager.Hand; int sum2 =0;
    foreach (var c in h2)
    {
        sum2 += Value(c.Value, h2);
    }
    if (sum2>=sum1)
    {
        return true;
    }
    else
        return false;

    return false;
}
```

any variables we could rename?

any duplication in terms of functionality?

any unnecessary logic or code?

A good place to start while doing any refactoring is to make sure all our variable and method names are good. So, why don't we start by cleaning those up first?

```
public bool DealerWins(Hand playerHand) {

    int playerHandValue = 0;

    foreach (var card in playerHand)
    {
        playerHandValue += DetermineCardValue(card, playerHand);
    }

    var dealerHand = DealerManager.Hand;
    int dealerHandValue= 0;

    foreach (var card in dealerHand)
    {
        dealerHandValue += DetermineCardValue(card, dealerHand);
    }

    return dealerHandValue >= playerHandValue;

}
```

Refactoring: [Rename variable]

Refactoring: [Rename method]

Refactoring: Simplified the code

Well, that's looking a bit better. It's a little more readable. But we aren't done yet. There is still some more duplication in there. What if we tried extracting some similar-looking logic into its own method?

```
public bool DealerWins(Hand playerHand)
{
    int playerHandValue = GetHandValue(playerHand);
    int dealerHandValue = GetHandValue(DealerManager.Hand);

    return dealerHandValue >= playerHandValue;
}
```

Refactoring: [Extract method]

```
private int GetHandValue(Hand hand)
{
    int handValue = 0;

    foreach (var card in hand)
    {
        handValue += DetermineCardValue(card, hand);
    }
    return handValue;
}
```

```
}
```

Wow! Look at that. After extracting the GetPlayerHandValue method, our DealerWins method collapsed down to just three lines. Now we can see what that method was trying to do. This is much easier to read. And if we ever want to see the details of how the player's hand is calculated, we can always drop down into the GetPlayerHandValue method and take a look.

This code is pretty clear. If we wanted to take it to the next level, of course, we could also do something like this:

Refactoring: [Inline variable]

```
public bool DealerWins(Hand playerHand)
{
    return GetHandValue(DealerManager.Hand) >= GetHandValue(playerHand);
}
```

With just these three simple refactorings:

- Rename variable/method
- Inline variable
- Extract method

you can really improve the readability and maintainability of your code.

For any managers out there reading this, this is important because now when the team needs to do that emergency bug fix or make that mission-critical change, they are going to be able to do it better, faster, and cheaper than before.

Instead of spending countless hours trying to figure out what the code is doing, they can get right to work and make the change.

For this reason, you should be a big supporter and cheerleader for ensuring the programmers on your team are aggressively refactoring and continuously paying down any technical debt.

Great question. Sometimes we do need to make bigger changes to our software than simply renaming a few variables. A library or framework may need to be replaced, a new tool may need to be integrated, or we believed the marketing hype a little too much and now need to replace a tool we were relying on for some heavy lifting.

Whatever the reason, big refactorings do come up from time to time, and we need a way to handle them.

If the change is imposed from outside the team and is something we just need to do, treat the refactoring like any other user story. Estimate it, prioritize it, make the cost visible, and show the impact it's going to have on the project.

Migrate to new corporate
security model

10 pts

big refactoring

Refactoring Gets a Dirty Name

Once, while building an energy-trading application, our team went off and did several large-scale refactorings in the code base and didn't add much in the way of new functionality for several weeks.

Well, it didn't take long for management to come to despise the word *refactoring* (because it came to mean rework and not adding any new functionality), and soon the edicts came from above that thou shalt not refactor.

Don't let this happen to you. Refactor continuously as you go. It's much harder to pay down the technical debt later, and the last thing you want to do is give refactoring a dirty name.

The trickier ones to handle are those more subjective cases where we could get by if we kept soldiering on, but the payback of doing this one change could really pay dividends down the road.

If your big refactoring falls into this gray area, ask yourself two questions before deciding whether to proceed:

- Are we near the end of the project?
- Can it be done incrementally?

Big end-of-project refactorings usually aren't worth the pain because you won't have time to reap the rewards of your work. So, it's usually a good idea to pass if you are near the end of your project.

Incremental refactorings are easier to sell to your customer because it means you and the team aren't going to disappear on them. They will continue to see new functionality in their software while you chip away at the refactoring incrementally.

Just take a look at your situation. See what needs to be done. And if it looks like it's going to save you a lot of pain, go for it—it's probably worth doing.

Where Can I Learn More?

We've only scratched the surface on the very important topic of refactoring, and this small chapter does not do the subject anywhere near the justice it deserves.

The book you really want to read is Martin Fowler's *Refactoring: Improving the Design of Existing Code* [FBB099].

Another worth reading is Michael Feathers' *Working Effectively with Legacy Code* [Fea04].

Master Sensei and the aspiring warrior

STUDENT: *Master, is there ever a time I shouldn't refactor my code?*

MASTER: *Save for the large-scale refactorings we already discussed, no. You generally want to refactor your code every time you make a change to the software.*

STUDENT: *Have I failed if I ever need an iteration dedicated to nothing but refactoring?*

MASTER: *No—it is just less than ideal. Try hard to do your refactorings in the small so you don't need to do them in the large. You won't always be successful, and large changes are sometimes required. But try to make them a last resort. It's not something you do regularly.*

What's Next?

Good stuff. Unit testing and refactoring together form a powerful one-two punch that most poorly designed software can't stand up against.

But there is another practice you need to know about—one that not only helps you with your software's design but also helps you figure out just how much to test.

Turn the page to discover the art of test-driven development and to see how writing tests first aids us as we stare at our blank canvas of code and wonder where it should all begin.

CHAPTER 14

Test-Driven Development

You're stuck. Stumped. You've been staring at one particular piece of code all day, and you just don't know how to break it down or even where to begin.

You wish you could code like Eric.

There is something about his code. It just seems to work. Whenever you use any of his code, it's like he has read your mind. Everything you need is right there—backed by a full suite of automated unit tests.

How does he do it? What's he doing that you're not?

Growing frustrated but realizing you need help, you finally muster up the courage and head over to Eric's desk. "How do you write such good, clean code?"

"Easy," he replies. "I write the tests first."

14.1 Write Your Tests First

Test-driven development (TDD) is a software development technique that uses really short development cycles to incrementally design your software.

Here's how it works:

1. *Red*: Before you write any new code for the system, you first write a failing unit test, showing the intent of what you would like the new code to do. Here you are thinking critically about the design.

2. *Green*: Then you do whatever it takes to make the test pass. If you see the full implementation, add the new code. If you don't, do just enough to get the test to pass.

3. *Refactor*: Then you go back and clean up any code or sins you committed while trying to get the test to pass. Here you are removing duplication and making sure everything is lean, mean, and as clear as possible.

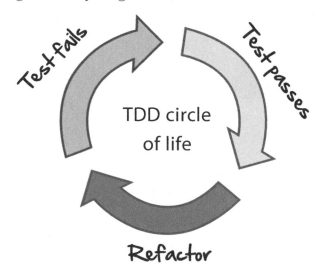

When asked how he knows when to stop, Eric replies that he keeps repeating the process of writing tests, making them pass, and refactoring until he's confident the code does everything the user story requires (usually this means passing all the story's acceptance criteria).

He also has a few rules of thumb for helping himself stay on track.

Rule #1: Don't write any new code until you first have a failing test.

Eric readily admits he isn't able to follow this rule 100 percent of the time (some stuff is just really hard to test first—like user interfaces). But the spirit of it, he explains, is not to write any more code than absolutely necessary. Writing a test first forces us to think about the value of what we are adding and helps prevent us from over-engineering the solution.

Rule #2: Test everything that could "possibly" break.

Following this rule doesn't mean you literally test *everything*—that would take forever. The key word here is *possibly*. If there is a plausible chance that something might break or we want to show intent in how the program will behave under certain conditions, we write a test for it. Eric then shows you an example of something he is currently working on.

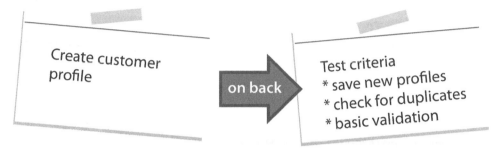

"As you know, we've got some real high rollers here in Vegas," Eric explains. "Something our data warehouse guys like to do is profile the movers and shakers. They figure out their likes, dislikes, favorite foods, favorite drinks, and anything else that can help us get them back to our casino.

"Now, we already have a customer profile object in the system. What I need to do is figure out how to store that profile information in the database."

The first thing Eric does is write a test. Here he imagines the code he needs to test already exists, and he is simply writing a test to prove to himself that it works:

```
tdd/test/CustomerProfileManagerTest.cs
[Test]
public void Create_Customer_Profile()
{
    // setup
    var manager = new CustomerProfileManager();

    // create a new customer profile
    var profile = new CustomerProfile("Scotty McLaren", "Hagis");

    // confirm it does not exist in the database
    Assert.IsFalse(manager.Exists(profile.Id));
```

```
    // add it
    int uniqueId = manager.Add(profile); // get id from database
    profile.Id = uniqueId;

    // confirm it's been added
    Assert.IsTrue(manager.Exists(uniqueId));

    // clean up
    manager.Remove(uniqueId);
}
```

Confident his test will tell him whether he can safely add a new customer profile, he then switches gears and now focuses on getting the test to pass.

Here he clearly sees what needs to be done (take the customer profile information and store it in the database), so he goes ahead and adds the new functionality.

tdd/src/CustomerProfileManager.cs
```
public class CustomerProfileManager
{

    public int Add(CustomerProfile profile)
    {
        // pretend this code stored the profile
        // in the database, and returned a real id
        return 0;
    }

    public bool Exists(int id)
    {
        // code to check if customer exists
    }

    public void Remove(int id)
    {
        // code to remove a customer from the database
    }
}
}
```

He now runs the test and sees that it passes. Yay!

Refactoring is the final leg of his TDD journey. He now goes back and looks over everything (test code, production code, configuration files, and whatever else he touched to make the test pass) and refactors it all really hard (Chapter 13, *Refactoring: Paying Down Your Technical Debt*, on page 195).

After refactoring, he goes back and asks himself whether he's tested everything that could possibly break. For this story, he needs to verify we don't allow any duplicates.

So, he repeats the same process. Write a failing test, do enough to make it pass, and then refactor.

Sometimes he has a bit of a chicken-and-egg problem (before he can test whether inserting works, he needs code that tells him whether the customer already exists).

When that happens, he just puts his current test on hold, adds the new functionality (testing first, of course), and then comes back to whatever it was he was working on before.

You thank Eric for his TDD demo and head back to your desk with thoughts of tests, refactoring, and code buzzing through your head.

What Just Happened Here?

Let's just stop and reflect for a second on what just happened here and why it's important.

In TDD we write the tests first, and then we make them pass. This seems backward. It's definitely not what we were taught in school.

But think about it for a second. What better way to design your software than to imagine it already exists!

That's all we are doing with TDD. Programmers write the code they need as if it already exists and then test to make sure it works. It's a wonderful way to ensure that you build only that which you need while testing that it works.

Now don't panic if your team doesn't suddenly take to TDD like a fish to water. It's a more advanced coding technique that builds on unit testing and refactoring. And to be sure, there will be times when you can't do TDD and you will just want to sit down and hack to figure stuff out.

But once you've got the basics and you experience the rhythm and power that comes from writing a small test, making it pass, and then refactoring, you'll like the way your code looks and tests.

14.2 Use the Tests to Deal with Complexity

Developers face a lot of complexity when writing code. Look at how many decisions Eric made when fleshing out his "Create customer profile" application programming interface (API).

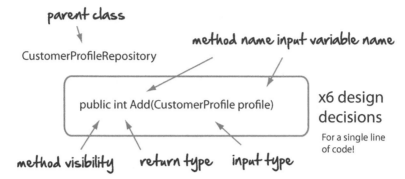

Count 'em. That's six design decisions, trade-offs, and forks in the road the developer needs to think about—all for a single line of code! It's no wonder things periodically fall through the cracks.

By writing your tests first and ensuring you have a failing test *before* adding the new code, TDD helps you fight the sheer amount of complexity you and your team are going to face writing code every day.

TDD also gives you a way of designing with confidence. By focusing on a single test and making it pass, you don't have to keep a thousand things in your head at once. You can focus on one little problem, learn incrementally how to best tackle it, and get the instant feedback you need to tell you whether you are headed in the right direction.

Other reasons for doing test-first include the following:

All of this makes for a much easier code base to maintain and modify. With less code comes less complexity. And with a simpler design, making changes and modifications becomes a lot easier.

Enough talk already. Let's drive some tests and see how you do on the test track.

Now you try

Eric invites you over to pair with him in writing some code that compares the value of two cards. He thinks the functionality should go in the Card class and would like your help fleshing out the test.

Write the method name you would like to see on the Card class that compares two cards and tells whether one is greater than the other.

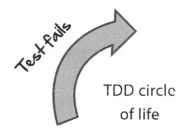

TDD circle of life

public void Compare value of two cards() {

    Card twoOfClubs = Card.TWO_OF_CLUBS;
    Card threeOfDiamonds = Card.THREE_OF_DIAMONDS;

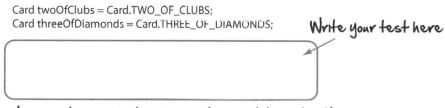

Write your test here

Imagine the code already exists – just type it out!

}

Say your design looks something like this:

```
tdd/test/CardTest.cs
[Test]
public void Compare_value_of_two_cards()
{
    Card twoOfClubs = Card.TWO_OF_CLUBS;
    Card threeOfDiamonds = Card.THREE_OF_DIAMONDS;

    Assert.IsTrue(twoOfClubs.IsLessThan(threeOfDiamonds));
}
```

Handing you the keyboard, Eric asks if you can make the test pass. You come up with something like this:

tdd/src/Card.cs
```
public bool IsLessThan(Card newCard)
{
    int thisCardValue = value;
    int newCardValue = newCard.value;
    return thisCardValue < newCardValue;
}
```

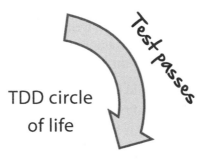

TDD circle
of life

After making the test pass, Eric asks you if you see anything you would like to refactor. You do. After making a few changes to the tests and the method, your code now looks something like this:

tdd/test/CardTest.cs
```
[Test]
public void Compare_value_of_two_card()
{
    Assert.IsTrue(Card.TWO_OF_CLUBS.IsLessThan(Card.THREE_OF_DIAMONDS));
}
```

tdd/src/Card.cs
```
public bool IsLessThan(Card newCard)
{
    return value < newCard.value;
}
```

TDD circle
of life

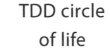

Refactor

After completing one loop of the TDD circle, Eric smiles and says, "I think you got it!" Keen to try this out on some of your own code, you thank Eric and head back to your desk to write some tests of your own.

Where Can I Learn More?

To really get the spirit of TDD, I recommend Kent Beck's book *Test Driven Development: By Example [Bec02]*, which has some good tips and tricks about the deeper mechanics of TDD and how to make it work for you.

Master Sensei and the aspiring warrior

STUDENT: *Master, I am confused about TDD. How am I supposed to write tests for code that doesn't even exist?*

MASTER: *Write the test as if the code you needed was already there.*

STUDENT: *But how will I know what to test?*

MASTER: *Test for that which you need.*

STUDENT: *So, you are saying to just write tests for things I need, and everything the system needs will magically appear.*

MASTER: *Yes.*

STUDENT: *Can you elaborate a little on exactly how all this magic works?*

MASTER: *There is no magic. You are simply manifesting that which you need in the form of a test. Creating code this way ensures you create only that which you need. You are simply using the tests as a gateway to realize your intent. This is why TDD is often referred to as a design technique and is less about testing.*

STUDENT: *So, TDD is really about design and not testing?*

MASTER:

That would be an oversimplification. Testing is a core part of TDD, because we use tests to prove that the code we produce works. But we cannot complete the tests without first doing some design and showing our intent through the code.

STUDENT: *Thank you, Master. I must think on this more.*

What's Next?

Can you feel the practices building? Unit testing gives us the confidence to know what we have built works. Refactoring ensures we keep it simple, and TDD gives us a powerful tool for dealing with complexity and design.

All that is left now is the one practice to bring them all together and ensure that your project is in a continual state of production readiness.

Let's now conclude and harness the power of continuous integration!

CHAPTER 15

Continuous Integration: Making It Production-Ready

Get ready for some production-ready goodness. By learning how to continuously integrate your software, you'll squash bugs early, lower the cost of making changes to your software, and be able to deploy with confidence.

And it looks like you need to do exactly that right now!

15.1 Showtime

First the good news. Your director is bringing by some influential investors to check out the latest version of your flagship Black Jack product. The bad news is they are going to be here in an hour!

That leaves you less than sixty minutes to create a stable build, push it onto the test server, and prepare for the demo.

What do you do?

Before you answer that, spend two minutes thinking of all the things that can go wrong whenever we deploy our software.

Things that can go wrong deploying software

Human error/fat fingers/bugs
Miscommunication with other teams
Errors / mistakes in configuration files
Differences in deployment environments
Out-of-date documentation

These are the things we want to eliminate, or at least manage, with our continuous integration process. We want to create a culture of production readiness and be able to demo our product to anyone, anytime, anywhere.

Let's look at two ways we could do this.

Scenario 1: The Big Production

One hour! That doesn't leave you much time. Hitting the panic button, you immediately pull the team together and, like a machine gun, start firing questions:

Who has the latest build?
Whose desktop is most stable?
Who can get something up and running in the shortest period of time?

Not trusting anyone to do this right but yourself, you inform everyone that your box will become the integration box for the demo and they all have fifteen minutes to merge their changes to your code branch.

As people start merging their code, more problems arise. Interfaces on core classes have changed. Configuration files have been modified. Files from the old system have been refactored out and are missing. Merging all the changes at once quickly becomes an integration nightmare.

Silently cursing the director for not giving you enough time, you tell people to comment out and hack around anything preventing them from integrating their code.

Then with five minutes to spare, you see a faint glimmer of hope—it compiles!

But then disaster—the investors show up five minutes early. No time to test.

Crossing your fingers, you deploy the software, fire up the application for the demo, and...it crashes. You fix that problem quickly and fire up the application, only to have it crash again after you make it through the introductory splash screen.

Slightly embarrassed and seeing the demo isn't going as expected, the director asks the team if they could maybe see some mock-ups instead.

Scenario 2: The Nonevent

Knowing you have a full hour before the demo, you give the team the heads-up that there is going to be a demo shortly and tell them that if they could check in and wrap up whatever it is they are working on, that would be greatly appreciated.

Once everyone's work has been saved, you check out the latest version of the code, run all the tests, and seeing that everything works, push it to test. The process is fully automated and takes about five minutes.

The investors arrive early. The demo goes great. And your boss thanks you for being able to present on such short notice and hands you something you've always wanted—the keys to the executive washroom.

OK, maybe you don't want the keys to the washroom, but you get the point.

Getting ready for demos and pushing code into production doesn't have to be a stressful, laborious, anxiety-filled big event.

You want the building, integrating, and deploying of your software to be a nonevent. And to do that, all you need is a nice smooth continuous integration process and a culture of production readiness.

15.2 A Culture of Production Readiness

There is a saying in Extreme Programming that production starts on day one of the project. From the first day you write a line of code, you treat the project as if it were in production, and after that, you are merely making changes to a live system.

It's a profound difference in how you view your code. Instead of viewing production and deployment as some event way off in the distant future, you imagine you and your team are in production today and start behaving accordingly.

Agilists like this notion of production readiness because it acknowledges that software spends a lot more time in production than development, and it gets the teams used to the idea of making changes to a production-ready system.

Maintaining a culture of production readiness isn't easy or free, however. It takes extreme discipline, and the temptation to delay investing in production-quality code in the name of schedule can be great.

But those who do make the investment early can turn their projects on a dime. They deploy with ease, make changes to their systems regularly and confidently, and respond to their customers' needs faster than their competitors can.

And something that helps us do that is continuous integration.

15.3 What Is Continuous Integration?

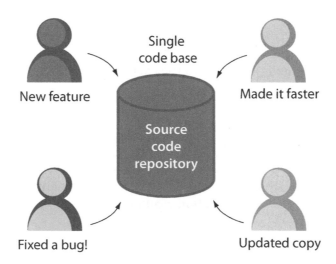

Continuous integration is the act of continuously taking changes developers make to their software and integrating them all together continuously throughout the day.

To use a book writing analogy, imagine you and your coauthor are working on a chapter together, and you need to merge your changes with hers. Merging some simple edits for a couple sentences isn't too bad.

The brown fox jumps over the lazy dog.

 Piece of cake ...

The brown fox jumps over the lazy *black* dog.

It's when we don't integrate our changes for extended periods of time that we run into trouble.

The brown fox jumps over the lazy dog. But
then the dog did something utterly amazing!
He baked a batch of chocolate chip cookies
and proceeded to hand deliver them to everyone
he passed on the street. The cats of course
saw this, got angry, and decided to counter the
dog's good will cookie campaign with a
campaign of their own   chocolate cheesecake!

 *Can you spot the
7 differences?*

The brown fox jumps over the lazy dog. But
then the dog did something utterly amazing!
He made a batch of chocolate chip muffins
and proceeded to deliver them to everyone
he passed on the avenue. The cats, of course
saw this, got angry and decided to counter the
dog's good will muffin campaign with a
campaign of their own—vanilla cheesecake!

Writing software is the same. The longer you go without integrating your changes with your teammates, the harder the merge is when you do.

Let's now see how this works in practice.

Keep It Quick

I was once on a project that had a great record/playback test automation tool. It was so great, in fact, that everyone started using it to record all their tests, and they stopped writing the faster, lower-level unit tests.

This was OK for a while, but as more record/playback tests accumulated, our automated build time jumped from a relatively nice quick ten minutes to just over three hours.

This killed us. People stopped running the build. They started checking in their work less often, and broken builds became the norm for the project.

Don't make the mistake we made of letting our builds get too long. Keep an eye on your build time. Anything under ten minutes is a good rule of thumb. Smaller projects can usually keep it to under five.

15.4 How Does It Work?

To set up a continuous integration system, you need a few things:

- A source code repository
- A check-in process
- An automated build
- A willingness to work in small chunks

Source code repositories store and version your software. This is what your development team "checks" their code into. It is the integration point of your project and keeps a master copy of your code. Open source repositories like Git or Subversion are your friends here.

Just make sure you avoid pessimistic locking (which means that only one developer can work on a file at a single time). It will frustrate your developers, slow your team down, and prevent your team from collectively owning the code base.

A good check-in process is more interesting. Let's see how a typical agile team might do that.

15.5 Establish a Check-in Process

A typical check-in process for developers working on an agile team would look something like this:

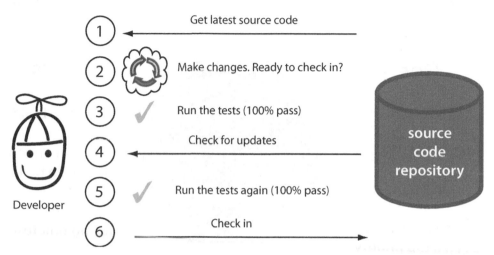

1. Get latest source from the repository.

Before you start any new work, you need to make sure you have the latest and greatest code from the repository. Here you check out the latest build and start your work with a clean slate.

2. Make changes.

Then you do your work. You add the new functionality, fix the bug, or do whatever work needs to be done.

3. Run tests.

To make sure the changes you made haven't broken something else in the code base, you run all your tests to make sure they all still pass.

4. Check for any more updates.

Confident your changes are working, you then get another update from the repository, just in case someone else made some changes while you were doing your work.

5. Run tests again.

Then you run the tests one more time to make sure your changes work with whatever other changes others have made since you started working.

6. Check-in.

All systems go. Everything builds. All the tests run. We've got the latest. It's safe to check in.

In addition to this check-in process, there are a couple dos and don'ts around good build conduct.

Dos

Check for updates

Run all the tests

Check in regularly

Make fixing a broken build a top priority

Don'ts

Break the build

Check in on top of broken builds

Comment out failing unit tests

At the end of the day, it's all about respecting the build, ensuring it's always up and running, and helping each other out when we break it (which happens from time to time).

15.6 Create an Automated Build

The next step is to create an automated build. It really forms the backbone of your team's continuous integration process.

A good automated build compiles the code, runs the tests, and basically does anything that regularly needs to be done as part of the project's build process.

Developers run it all the time as part of the TDD circle of life, and build agents (like CruiseControl[1]) use it to run the build whenever they detect a change in the source code repository.

---

1. http://cruisecontrol.sourceforge.net/

Developers

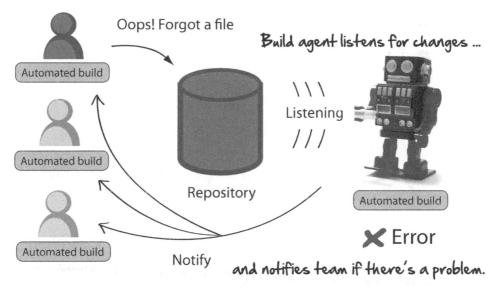

Automated builds can also automate deploying the software into production and remove a lot of the human error from that equation.

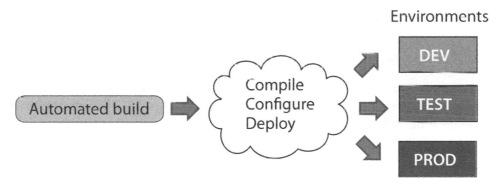

The key to any build is automation—the less human involvement, the better. You also want to keep your build fast, because you and your team are going to be running constantly, many times per day (under ten minutes is a good rule of thumb).

Most modern languages have their own automated build frameworks (Ant for Java, NAnt or MS-Build for .NET, and rake for Rails). If the language you are using doesn't, you can usually create your own with DOS bat files or Unix scripts.

But as good as check-in processes and automated builds are, what really makes it all work is a willingness to work in small chunks.

15.7 Work in Small Chunks

Just like testing with TDD, integrating code is much easier when done in the small.

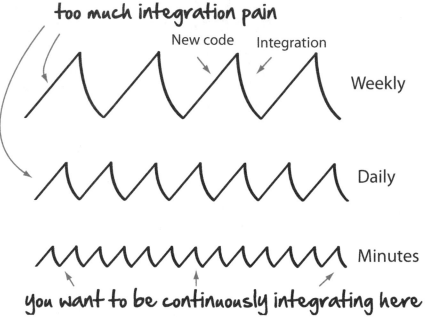

Too often teams go for days or weeks without integrating their work—that's way too long. You want to be integrating your code every ten to fifteen minutes or so (at a minimum on the hour).

Don't get stressed if you can't check in that often. Just understand that the more you do it, the easier it gets. So, merge your code early and often to avoid the pain of big integrations.

Where Can I Learn More?

Continuous integration has become such a common practice that you can find just about everything you'll need on the Web.

Wikipedia has a good summary of the practice,[2] and one of the first continuous integration articles can be found on Martin Fowler's website.[3]

---

2.   http://en.wikipedia.org/wiki/Continuous_integration
3.   http://martinfowler.com/articles/continuousIntegration.html

Master Sensei and the aspiring warrior

STUDENT: *Master, we obviously can't have everything production-ready during the first iteration. What do you really mean when you say "production-ready"?*

MASTER: *Production readiness is an attitude. When you write production-ready code, you test and integrate your software today. When you see a bug, you fix it now. You don't sweep it under the carpet and imagine getting to it at some distant point in the future. You take the attitude that this software has to work today. Not the distant tomorrow. Yes, you may not have every bell and whistle you would like, and yes, you may choose not to deploy until more features are added. But having the option to deploy, and knowing your software works, is to accept that your software will spend the vast majority of its life in production (not development) and gets you used to the thought of making changes to a live production system.*

STUDENT: *What if I can't build the whole system because my project is just one small piece of the bigger picture?*

MASTER: *Then build, test, and deploy what you can. At some point, you will need to integrate your piece with everything else. Do your best to make sure your portion is ready so you will be able to make the necessary changes when you can. But don't let the fact that you are one small piece stop you from automating your build or continuously integrating your software.*

That's All Folks!

So, there you have it. Our tour de force of essential agile software engineering practices:

- Unit testing—to prove that what we built works

- Refactoring—the art of simplicity and keeping the code clean and a joy to read

- Test-driven development (TDD)—for designing and dealing with complexity

- Continuous integration—regularly bringing it all together and maintaining a state of production readiness

Without these, little on our agile projects would work, and we would quickly revert to our caveman days of "code and fix."

15.8   Where Do I Go from Here?

Congratulations! You are now armed and dangerous with the knowledge and know-how to kick off, plan, and execute your very own agile project.

Where you go from here is entirely up to you.

If you are starting a new project, maybe you want to kick things off with an inception deck (Chapter 3, *How to Get Everyone on the Bus*, on page 35). Get everyone on the bus and headed in the right direction by asking the tough questions right at the start of the project.

Or, if you are already in the middle of a project (and your plan is clearly wrong), maybe you'll hit the reset button by hosting a story-gathering workshop (Section 6.4, *How to Host a Story-Gathering Workshop*, on page 93), picking a few really important stories, and seeing whether you can deliver a few of those every week. Then build a new plan based on that.

Or, if you are hurting on the engineering side, maybe you start by looking at some of your engineering practices and make sure you're not cutting corners on the testing and are regularly paying down your technical debt.

There is no map. You are going to have to figure out what is best for you and your project. But understand that you have the tools, and I bet you probably already know what needs to be done.

What's stopping you?
Get out there and start doing it!

Final Words

It's all about choice.

No one can stop you from producing high-quality software. No one can stop you from being up front and honest with your customers about the state of your project and what needs to be done.

Don't get me wrong—none of this is easy. We have decades of history and baggage working against us. But at the end of the day, understand that how you choose to work, and the quality of the work you produce, is up to you and no one else.

Don't evangelize.
Don't tell other people what to do.
Instead, lead by example, accept that others won't always be there, and do what needs to be done.

Oh yeah, and one more thing.

Don't Worry About Being Agile

One question you hear a lot from teams when they first get into agile is, "Are we there yet? Are we being agile?"

And that's a fair question to ask. Like doing anything new for the first time, you're naturally going to want to know how you are doing and whether you are doing it by the book.

And that's totally cool. Just understand there is no book—not this one or any other—that I or anyone else can give you that will tell you whether you are being agile.

It's not a checklist. It's a journey, not a destination. You never really get there.

And don't forget. It's not about "being" agile. It's about building great products and delivering world class service to your customers.

All I can say is if you think you've made it and you've got it all figured out, you've stopped being agile.

So, don't get hung up on the practices. Take what you can from this book, and make it fit your unique situation and context. And whenever you are wondering whether you are doing things the "agile way," instead ask yourself two questions:

- Are we delivering something of value every week?
- Are we striving to continuously improve?

If you can answer yes to both those questions, you're being agile.

Part VI

Appendixes

Agile Principles

Here's a summary of the Agile Manifesto[1] and twelve guiding principles of the agile software movement[2] taken from the Agile Manifesto website.

A1.1 The Agile Manifesto

We are uncovering better ways of developing software by doing it and helping others do it. Through this work we have come to value:

Individuals and interactions over processes and tools
Working software over comprehensive documentation
Customer collaboration over contract negotiation
Responding to change over following a plan

That is, while there is value in the items on the right, we value the items on the left more.

A1.2 Twelve Agile Principles

1. Our highest priority is to satisfy the customer through early and continuous delivery of valuable software.

2. Welcome changing requirements, even late in development. Agile processes harness change for the customer's competitive advantage.

3. Deliver working software frequently, from a couple of weeks to a couple of months, with a preference to the shorter timescale.

---

1. http://agilemanifesto.org
2. http://agilemanifesto.org/principles.html

4. Businesspeople and developers must work together daily throughout the project.

5. Build projects around motivated individuals. Give them the environment and support they need, and trust them to get the job done.

6. The most efficient and effective method of conveying information to and within a development team is face-to-face conversation.

7. Working software is the primary measure of progress.

8. Agile processes promote sustainable development. The sponsors, developers, and users should be able to maintain a constant pace indefinitely.

9. Continuous attention to technical excellence and good design enhances agility.

10. Simplicity—the art of maximizing the amount of work not done—is essential.

11. The best architectures, requirements, and designs emerge from self-organizing teams.

12. At regular intervals, the team reflects on how to become more effective and then tunes and adjusts its behavior accordingly.

Resources

There are many great newsgroups, resources, and other places for you to continue your journey. Here are some good places to hang out and learn more about agile software delivery and how it works:

- http://tech.groups.yahoo.com/group/extremeprogramming

- http://groups.yahoo.com/group/scrumdevelopment

- http://tech.groups.yahoo.com/group/leanagile

- http://finance.groups.yahoo.com/group/kanbandev

- http://tech.groups.yahoo.com/group/agile-testing

- http://tech.groups.yahoo.com/group/agile-usability

- http://finance.groups.yahoo.com/group/agileprojectmanagement

Bibliography

[Bec00]   Kent Beck. *Extreme Programming Explained: Embrace Change*. Addison-Wesley Longman, Reading, MA, 2000.

[Bec02]   Kent Beck. *Test Driven Development: By Example*. Addison-Wesley, Reading, MA, 2002.

[Blo01]   Michael Bloomberg. *Bloomberg by Bloomberg*. John Wiley & Sons, New York, NY, 2001.

[CG08]   Lisa Crispin and Janet Gregory. *Agile Testing: A Practical Guide for Testers and Agile Teams*. Addison-Wesley, Reading, MA, 2008.

[Car90]   Dale Carnegie. *How to Win Friends and Influence People*. Pocket, New York, NY, USA, 1990.

[DC03]   Mark Denne and Jane Cleland Huang. *Software by Numbers: Low-Risk, High-Return Development*. Prentice Hall, Englewood Cliffs, NJ, 2003.

[DL06]   Esther Derby and Diana Larsen. *Agile Retrospectives: Making Good Teams Great*. The Pragmatic Bookshelf, Raleigh, NC and Dallas, TX, 2006.

[Eva03]   Eric Evans. *Domain-Driven Design: Tackling Complexity in the Heart of Software*. Addison-Wesley Longman, Reading, MA, First, 2003.

[FBBO99]   Martin Fowler, Kent Beck, John Brant, William Opdyke, and Don Roberts. *Refactoring: Improving the Design of Existing Code*. Addison-Wesley, Reading, MA, 1999.

[Fea04]   Michael Feathers. *Working Effectively with Legacy Code*. Prentice Hall, Englewood Cliffs, NJ, 2004.

[HH07]   Chip Heath and Dan Heath. *Made to Stick: Why Some Ideas Survive and Others Die*. Random House, New York, NY, USA, 2007.

[Joh98]   Spencer Johnson. *Who Moved My Cheese? An Amazing Way to Deal with Change in Your Work and in Your Life*. Putnam Publishing Group, Kirkwood, NY, USA, 1998.

[Lik04]   Jeffrey Liker. *The Toyota Way*. McGraw-Hill, Emeryville, CA, 2004.

[McC06]   Steve McConnell}. *Software Estimation: Demystifying the Black Art*. Microsoft Press, Redmond, WA, 2006.

[Moo91]   Geoffrey A. Moore. *Crossing the Chasm*. Harper Business, New York, NY, USA, 1991.

[SD09]   Rachel Sedley and Liz Davies. *Agile Coaching*. The Pragmatic Bookshelf, Raleigh, NC and Dallas, TX, 2009.

[Sch03]   David Schmaltz. *The Blind Men and the Elephant*. Berrett-Koehler, San Francisco, CA, USA, 2003.

[Sur05]   James Surowiecki. *The Wisdom of Crowds*. Anchor, New York, NY, USA, 2005.

[TH03]   David Thomas and Andrew Hunt. *Pragmatic Unit Testing In Java with JUnit*. The Pragmatic Bookshelf, Raleigh, NC and Dallas, TX, 2003.

[TH04]   David Thomas and Andrew Hunt. *Pragmatic Unit Testing In C# with NUnit*. The Pragmatic Bookshelf, Raleigh, NC and Dallas, TX, 2004.

Index

Be Agile

Don't just "do" agile; you want to *be* agile. We'll show you how.

The best agile book isn't a book: *Agile in a Flash* is a unique deck of index cards that fit neatly in your pocket. You can tape them to the wall. Spread them out on your project table. Get stains on them over lunch. These cards are meant to be used, not just read.

Jeff Langr and Tim Ottinger
(110 pages) ISBN: 9781934356715. $15
http://pragprog.com/titles/olag

You know the Agile and Lean development buzzwords, you've read the books. But when systems need a serious overhaul, you need to see how it works in real life, with real situations and people. *Lean from the Trenches* is all about actual practice. Every key point is illustrated with a photo or diagram, and anecdotes bring you inside the project as you discover why and how one organization modernized its workplace in record time.

Henrik Kniberg
(178 pages) ISBN: 9781934356852. $30
http://pragprog.com/titles/hklean

More on Agile Development

Working on embedded systems or on your own? This is how it's done, the agile way.

Still chasing bugs and watching your code deteriorate? Think TDD is only for desktop or web apps? It's not: TDD is for you, the embedded C programmer. TDD helps you prevent defects and build software with a long useful life. This is the first book to teach the hows and whys of TDD for C programmers.

James W. Grenning
(352 pages) ISBN: 9781934356623. $34.95
http://pragprog.com/titles/jgade

Want to be a better developer? This book collects the personal habits, ideas, and approaches of successful agile software developers and presents them in a series of short, easy-to-digest tips.

You'll learn how to improve your software development process, see what real agile practices feel like, avoid the common temptations that kill projects, and keep agile practices in balance.

Venkat Subramaniam and Andy Hunt
(208 pages) ISBN: 9780974514086. $29.95
http://pragprog.com/titles/pad

Refactor Your Career

Time to debug and refactor your career, and start doing it right. Start here.

Technical Blogging is the first book to specifically teach programmers, technical people, and technically-oriented entrepreneurs how to become successful bloggers. There is no magic to successful blogging; with this book you'll learn the techniques to attract and keep a large audience of loyal, regular readers and leverage this popularity to achieve your goals.

Antonio Cangiano
(288 pages) ISBN: 9781934356883. $33
http://pragprog.com/titles/actb

You're already a great coder, but awesome coding chops aren't always enough to get you through your toughest projects. You need these 50+ nuggets of wisdom. Veteran programmers: reinvigorate your passion for developing web applications. New programmers: here's the guidance you need to get started. With this book, you'll think about your job in new and enlightened ways.

This title is also available as an audio book.

Ka Wai Cheung
(160 pages) ISBN: 9781934356791. $29
http://pragprog.com/titles/kcdc

Get Results

Reading about new techniques is one thing, making them work in your company and on your team is another matter entirely. Here's the help you need.

If you work with people, you need this book. Learn to read co-workers' and users' *patterns of resistance* and dismantle their objections. With these techniques and strategies you can master the art of evangelizing and help your organization adopt your solutions.

Terrence Ryan
(146 pages) ISBN: 9781934356609. $32.95
http://pragprog.com/titles/trevan

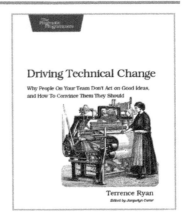

Discover how to coach your team to become more Agile. *Agile Coaching* de-mystifies agile practices—it's a practical guide to creating strong agile teams. Packed with useful tips from practicing agile coaches Rachel Davies and Liz Sedley, this book gives you coaching tools that you can apply whether you are a project manager, a technical lead, or working in a software team.

Rachel Davies and Liz Sedley
(250 pages) ISBN: 9781934356432. $34.95
http://pragprog.com/titles/sdcoach

Think Better

Want to concentrate more effectively, and learn how to take advantage of your brain's wiring? We've got you covered.

Do you ever look at the clock and wonder where the day went? You spent all this time at work and didn't come close to getting everything done. Tomorrow, try something new. Use the Pomodoro Technique, originally developed by Francesco Cirillo, to work in focused sprints throughout the day. In *Pomodoro Technique Illustrated*, Staffan Nöteberg shows you how to organize your work to accomplish more in less time. There's no need for expensive software or fancy planners. You can get started with nothing more than a piece of paper, a pencil, and a kitchen timer.

This title is also available as an audio book.

Staffan Nöteberg
(144 pages) ISBN: 9781934356500. $24.95
http://pragprog.com/titles/snfocus

Software development happens in your head. Not in an editor, IDE, or design tool. You're well educated on how to work with software and hardware, but what about *wetware*—our own brains? Learning new skills and new technology is critical to your career, and it's all in your head.

In this book by Andy Hunt, you'll learn how our brains are wired, and how to take advantage of your brain's architecture. You'll learn new tricks and tips to learn more, faster, and retain more of what you learn.

You need a pragmatic approach to thinking and learning. You need to *Refactor Your Wetware*.

Andy Hunt
(290 pages) ISBN: 9781934356050. $34.95
http://pragprog.com/titles/ahptl

The Pragmatic Bookshelf

The Pragmatic Bookshelf features books written by developers for developers. The titles continue the well-known Pragmatic Programmer style and continue to garner awards and rave reviews. As development gets more and more difficult, the Pragmatic Programmers will be there with more titles and products to help you stay on top of your game.

Visit Us Online

This Book's Home Page
http://pragprog.com/titles/jtrap
Source code from this book, errata, and other resources. Come give us feedback, too!

Register for Updates
http://pragprog.com/updates
Be notified when updates and new books become available.

Join the Community
http://pragprog.com/community
Read our weblogs, join our online discussions, participate in our mailing list, interact with our wiki, and benefit from the experience of other Pragmatic Programmers.

New and Noteworthy
http://pragprog.com/news
Check out the latest pragmatic developments, new titles and other offerings.

Save on the eBook

Save on the eBook versions of this title. Owning the paper version of this book entitles you to purchase the electronic versions at a terrific discount.

PDFs are great for carrying around on your laptop—they are hyperlinked, have color, and are fully searchable. Most titles are also available for the iPhone and iPod touch, Amazon Kindle, and other popular e-book readers.

Buy now at *http://pragprog.com/coupon*

Contact Us

Online Orders:	*http://pragprog.com/catalog*
Customer Service:	*support@pragprog.com*
International Rights:	*translations@pragprog.com*
Academic Use:	*academic@pragprog.com*
Write for Us:	*http://pragprog.com/write-for-us*
Or Call:	+1 800-699-7764

CPSIA information can be obtained at www.ICGtesting.com
Printed in the USA
BVOW10s1450171214

379835BV00006B/18/P